PRESENTED TO:

Judy

FROM:

Patti Peterson

DATE:

December 2020

PRAISE FOR
ANNE NEILSON'S ANGELS

"I have been a longtime fan of Anne's incredibly beautiful work. Her art transcends this earth and touches my soul. She is a true inspiration."

—MARIA SHRIVER, JOURNALIST, AUTHOR, FORMER FIRST LADY OF CALIFORNIA

"A devotional book filled with radiant angels bringing hope and peace when we need it most. In these pages filled with Anne's beautiful art and words, you will find inspiration to live a more meaningful life."

—JENNA BUSH HAGER, CO-HOST OF THE FOURTH HOUR OF *TODAY*

"Anything to which we give our attention will grow and flourish—the good and the bad. What a beautiful template Anne has created to cultivate an atmosphere of hope and beauty to start the day by inviting us to contemplate a single word. To see that word through the lens of understanding, to contemplate its meaning in light of Scripture, to see it illustrated through the stroke of her paint brush."

—AMY GRANT, SIX-TIME GRAMMY AWARD WINNER

"Michelangelo looked at marble and saw angels, then chipped away until he set them free. My dear friend Anne Neilson looks at a blank canvas and sees hope, faith, love, and encouragement. From deep in her soul she begins to add layers of texture and strokes of beautiful colors until angels appear. Then with the purity of white, she gives wings and sets the angels free to let God take care of the rest. Never in my fifty-year career as an art dealer have I seen art used for a greater purpose. Now in this extraordinarily beautiful devotional, your day can begin and end with angels and inspiring words that will penetrate your soul as God takes care of the rest."

—RON HALL, INTERNATIONAL ART DEALER, FILM PRODUCER,
AND AUTHOR OF *SAME KIND OF DIFFERENT AS ME*

"What a blessing this beautiful book of devotionals from Anne Neilson is. Her writing and her paintings speak beautifully to the soul. Each word is a gentle and wonderful reminder that angels are all around us, shining God's light on us and guiding us forward."

—ROMA DOWNEY, ACTRESS, PRODUCER, AND AUTHOR

"You are what you paint."

—JIMMY WAYNE, RECORDING ARTIST AND *NEW YORK TIMES* BESTSELLING AUTHOR

"We first met Anne when she sent us a beautiful painting after the loss of our daughter, Maria. There are no words to describe someone who prayed for your family with every brush stroke of her work. Anne has not only encouraged our family with her art, but with her words and the way she lives her life. Our prayer is that the words in this book penetrate deep within your soul and you feel the presence of God deeply. The way her paintings and her writings go hand in hand is such a gift to all of us. Again, as you ponder these words, know that Anne is someone who has been willing to give back her gifts to the One who is the giver of all gifts."

—MARY BETH AND STEVEN CURTIS CHAPMAN, FIVE-TIME GRAMMY AWARD WINNER

"Anne has a gift, a very beautiful and unusual gift. She brings tender words and profound images together and they speak louder than words or images alone ever could. This book is a treasure to tuck into your life for years to come."

—SHEILA WALSH, AUTHOR OF *PRAYING WOMEN* AND *PRAYING GIRLS DEVOTIONAL*

"Anne is a brilliant artist with a gift from God! Her masterpieces remind us of God's protection and safety! Her devotional will help you reflect on His constant awareness and His goodness."

—NICOLE C. MULLEN, SINGER, SONGWRITER, AND CHOREOGRAPHER

"This book is a gift to the world. Whether you are feeling weary or living your fullest life, Anne's words and paintings will bring you so much joy, comfort, and inspiration. Every page is filled with a light that has stayed with me even after I closed the book. It's a beautiful reminder that angels are always with us and one I'll read over and over."

—MALLORY ERVIN, FOUNDER AND CEO OF LIVE FULLY BRAND,
     HOST OF *LIVING FULLY* PODCAST, AND AUTHOR

"Anne Neilson's work is inspiring and lovely. Her art is a feast for the eyes and her words are food for your soul!"

—AMY HANNON, OWNER OF EUNA MAE'S AND AUTHOR OF *LOVE
     WELCOME SERVE: RECIPES THAT GATHER AND GIVE*

ANNE NEILSON'S
Angels

DEVOTIONS AND ART TO ENCOURAGE, REFRESH, AND INSPIRE

ANNE NEILSON

THOMAS NELSON
Since 1798

Published in Nashville, Tennessee, by Thomas Nelson. Thomas Nelson is a registered trademark of HarperCollins Christian Publishing, Inc.

Thomas Nelson titles may be purchased in bulk for educational, business, fund-raising, or sales promotional use. For information, please email SpecialMarkets@ThomasNelson.com.

Unless otherwise noted, Scripture quotations are taken from the Holy Bible, New International Version®, NIV®. Copyright © 1973, 1978, 1984, 2011 by Biblica, Inc.® Used by permission of Zondervan. All rights reserved worldwide. www.zondervan.com. The "NIV" and "New International Version" are trademarks registered in the United States Patent and Trademark Office by Biblica, Inc.®

Scripture quotations marked CEV are from The Holy Bible, Contemporary English Version. Copyright © 1995 American Bible Society. All rights reserved.

Scripture quotations marked ESV are from The ESV® Bible (The Holy Bible, English Standard Version®), copyright © 2001 by Crossway, a publishing ministry of Good news Publishers. Used by permission. All rights reserved.

Scripture quotations marked KJV are from King James Version. Public domain.

Scripture quotations marked NASB are from the New American Standard Bible®. Copyright © 1960, 1962, 1963, 1968, 1971, 1972, 1973, 1975, 1977, 1995 by The Lockman Foundation. Used by permission. (www.Lockman.org)

Scripture quotations marked NKJV are from the New King James Version®. © 1982 by Thomas Nelson. Used by permission. All rights reserved.

Scripture quotations marked NLT are from the Holy Bible, New Living Translation. Copyright © 1996, 2004, 2007, 2013, 2015 by Tyndale House Foundation. Used by permission of Tyndale House Publishers, Inc., Carol Stream, Illinois, 60188. All rights reserved.

The definitions of the forty key words in this book are from the Merriam-Webster online dictionary at https://www.merriam-webster.com/.

Art direction: Sabryna Lugge
Interior design: Mallory Collins

ISBN: 978-1-4402-2084-7 (eBook)
ISBN: 978-1-4002-2040-3 (Hardcover)

Printed in China

20 21 22 23 24 DSC 10 9 8 7 6 5 4 3 2 1

I dedicate this book to my family—
Clark, Blakely, Catherine, Taylor, and Ford.
You are my everything, and I pray that as you journey through life,
you will cling to the most powerful word: God's WORD and His promises.
Be encouraged—always!

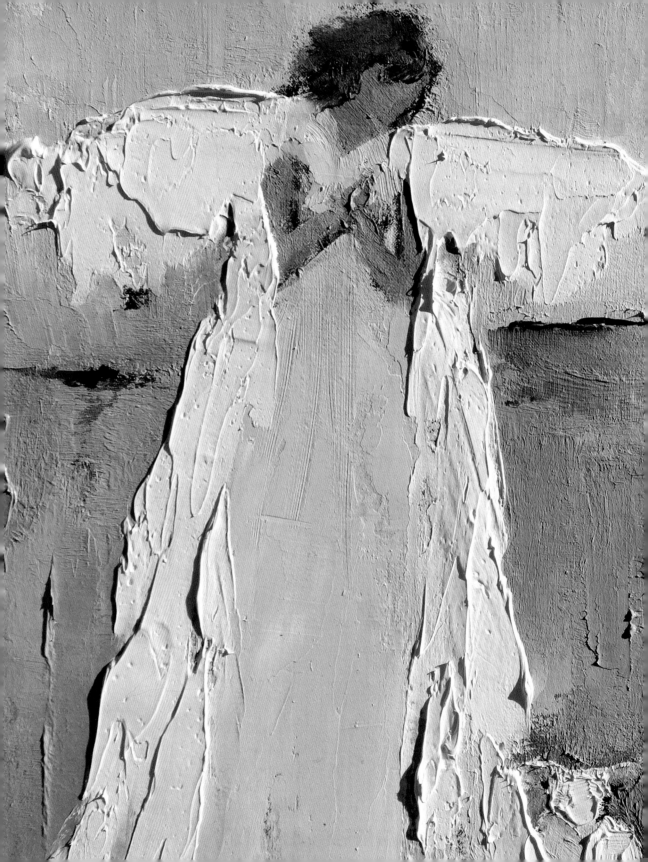

CONTENTS

FOREWORD

By Kathie Lee Gifford

I am blessed to know lots of blessed people. That's how God works: He creates a mosaic. He stitches a quilt. He weaves a tapestry.

He brought Anne into my life in 2013, when He knew we needed each other. I needed beauty and she needed encouragement. The very moment I saw the cover of her book *Angels in Our Midst*, it resonated as truth in my soul. Her art tells you everything you need to know about the woman who creates it, and the One who created her.

When Anne told me that she was working on a devotional, I was delighted at the thought of her angels being the perfect partner to the words of God's steadfast love and the knowledge that His angels are watching over us every moment of every day. I have some of her angel paintings in my foyer for a similar reason—to offer hope and to serve as a reminder that we are never alone, no matter what trials we may be facing. "For he will command his angels concerning you to guard you in all your ways" (Psalm 91:11).

Each morning I wake up at a ridiculously early hour, and instead of wishing I could fall back to sleep, I so look forward to my time alone with the Word of God. For years I've been reading the same devotionals and enjoy the daily reminders of God's faithfulness and encouragement for the day ahead. It's a cherished time to be alone with our Savior and His Word. I can't wait to add Anne's book to my morning routine. She is a living example of God's faithfulness and has used God's gifts to shower others with grace, love, and overwhelming generosity of both spirit and deeds.

Anne lives for Him, she paints for Him, and she rejoices in Him. But most of all, she is filled with purpose to *serve* Him.

Anne has become a dear friend, a cherished sister in Jesus Christ, and an anointed prayer warrior to me. I know that in her new devotional, *Anne Neilson's Angels*, her devotions and her art will encourage, refresh, and inspire you—drawing you closer to the Savior she loves. That is my prayer.

INTRODUCTION

*I*n 2003 I began my series of angel paintings on a piece of paper as sketches reflecting my faith. They soon evolved onto my canvas as ethereal abstract beings sculpted from oil paint.

Much like my paintings, which start out on a blank canvas, our life journey starts clean and fresh, then explodes in color and sweeping brushstrokes with each trial and tribulation we face. Through these experiences, whether joyful or difficult, God adds hue and texture to create a beautiful masterpiece.

My prayer is that the art and stories throughout this little book will be a beautiful reminder for you that God is both our Creator and the fulfiller of His promises to us.

I am so glad you have chosen this devotional. I am not sure how it landed in your hands—perhaps it was a gift from a friend, or maybe the angel on the cover captured your heart. Whatever the case may be, I pray that over the next forty days, or forty weeks, or however you choose to use this forty-word devotional, you will allow the ethereal angels and the personal stories to penetrate deep into your soul and bring a sense of wonder, peace, comfort, and healing, drawing you closer to our living Lord Jesus.

I pray that you will allow the ethereal angels and the personal stories to penetrate deep into your soul and bring a sense of wonder, peace, comfort, and healing, drawing you closer to our living Lord Jesus.

More than seventeen years ago, I painted my first little angel. I sent the angel image to my sister and asked her what she thought. "You have found your voice," she told me. I have discovered over the years that God has used these angels for His purpose and for *His* ministry on so many levels, and because of that, these paintings have become my life song.

In 2012 I self-published my first book, *Angels in Our Midst* (a large coffee-table book). I created the book simply because everyone wanted an "angel"—and God was orchestrating so many stories and divine appointments as I journeyed through my art career. Unfortunately, coffee-table books often become stacked several deep on beautiful tables in front of sofas, and rarely are these beautiful books opened.

Months into the release, I received an email from someone who had done just that. She bought the book to be an ornament on her table and did not even think to open it until one day when she felt prompted by the Holy Spirit. She spent the rest of her morning reading each chapter and then sent me an email, telling me that the book was her new devotional. In my response to her, I remarked that perhaps I should start working on a smaller, less awkward-to-handle devotional. That was seven years ago—and how this little devotional came to be.

It is funny and amazing how God works. He brings the right people into our lives at just the right time—in *His* timing.

So many devotional themes ran through my mind as I began writing. Frankly, I think of myself as a living, breathing, walking devotional, and I believe the Lord opens my eyes along my journey so I can see His mighty hand at work in my life daily.

Recently I was having a discussion with a friend who always chooses a word at the beginning of each January as a theme for the year. She told me that as she was lying on her yoga mat, meditating on which word she would choose for the year, she landed on *dread*. The Lord interrupted her and said her word would be *joy*. She said, "No—*dread*." He said, "No—*joy*!" This went on for several minutes, until she finally conceded to *joy*.

You see, her big sister, who also happened to be my best friend, had traveled home to Jesus just six months earlier. My friend dreaded what the new year would bring without her big sister. But God and His promises—which are always true—wanted her to know that *joy* was her word. And not just a trickle of joy; He brings *abundant* joy. Joy that overflows. Joy that can bring peace in the midst of chaos. Joy that can replace heartache. So now my friend will cling to *joy* this year.

I decided to do a devotional on words because words are so powerful. Think about my friend: if she had settled on the word *dread*, what might that have looked like as she navigated through life that year? In every thought pattern, in every conversation, in what she was going through in her daily life, she would be bringing dread with her, and likely missing out on all of God's blessings. I am so excited to share with you that we serve a living Jesus, and through the Holy Spirit He interrupts our thought processes and steps in. Praise God!

The power of words isn't completely new to me. Early on, I was convicted on how we use them. Words can either build someone up or tear someone down. Our thoughts are brought to life through language—the ways we think and act—each word deeply impacting how we live and breathe and view the world. Our thoughts cannot exist without words and language. (Go ahead. Try to formulate a thought without using words. It's literally impossible.) This is where the power lies—when we are intentional with our thoughts, we can speak out loud God's truths despite what we might be going through in life, and then we can begin to transform our thought patterns.

More than thirty years ago, I was a third-grade teacher who stepped into a wonderful class midway through the school year. The teacher who was leaving had a label for each child.

"This one is a studier."

"This one is a talker."

"This one is a troublemaker."

The first thing I did when I walked into that room was remove each of the labels she had placed on the children, and then I immediately began speaking words and phrases of affirmation over each one.

"This one is wonderfully and fearfully made."

"This one is a child of God."

"This one can do *all* things through Christ."

These words of affirmation were powerful and effective, and it was wonderful to see the transformation of these amazing children at the end of the school year.

You may already have a word you are clinging to for the year. I have many! This little book gives you forty more words, along with a glimpse of my journey, which I hope will encourage you daily.

My prayer is that you let the words on each page minister to you in whatever you might be going through. If you are in a season of despair, I pray you cling to *hope*. If you are experiencing a season of busyness, I pray that you pause and reflect on what is truly calling you.

My prayer is that you let the words on each page minister to you in whatever you might be going through.

By the way, as you read, you'll soon learn that *busy* is the number-one word people use to label me. I hear it all the time. I understand that my version of busy does not look like your version, and I never want to glorify that word. Instead, I want to shift the focus of what it means to be busy, because for me, it's more about service and using the gifts God gave me. In the meantime, don't let the world label you; choose your own word, and continue on your journey to a higher calling—for His kingdom.

Did I mention how important it is to carve out some time to sit with Jesus? When my first book came out, a young girl reached out to me to grab coffee and

chat. We met at the little local coffee shop, and she told me that she just wanted to know more. She said she knew I was "religious," and I stopped her there. Whoa, what a word! My faith and service to God are not about "religion" the way some people may think of it. My life is about cultivating a relationship with a living God through His Son, Jesus.

Some people become perplexed hearing this, which, admittedly, perplexes me. God created us for a relationship—an *intimate* relationship. We're not meant to simply go through the motions.

Think about Adam and Eve in the early days in the garden. They walked and talked with God daily. It wasn't until the fall—not the season, but the time that Adam and Eve disobeyed God and did exactly what God had told them not to do, and they ate that ripe, delicious piece of fruit—when their eyes were opened.

They were naked.

God came looking.

They hid.

Adam and Eve were ashamed, but God covered them. That was the first animal sacrifice that had ever taken place—to cover them. There's some pretty cool stuff in the Bible when we're willing to look a little deeper.

Back to words. I can use a lot of them here because it is so exciting to see how much God cares about us, even when we mess up. And He so desires to connect with us each day—and not just on our timetable. We have the ability to create and participate in a round-the-clock conversation with God.

I pray that you will use this little book filled with forty words and my art to center yourself in a position to chat with God. To pour out your heart. Your fears. Your challenges. Your hopes. Your dreams.

Whatever season of life you are experiencing, I offer these chosen words and artwork as a display and a reminder of the artful hand of our Creator at work in your life.

Love

/ˈləv/

noun

1. strong affection for another arising out of kinship or
    personal ties
2. warm attachment, enthusiasm, or devotion

verb

1. to hold dear; cherish

ONE

LOVE

We love because he first loved us.

1 John 4:19

---

*L*ove is such a peculiar word, isn't it? Both overused and incredibly difficult to define, yet we love to love things. You can love the meal you prepared for your family. You can fall madly in love with a romantic partner. You can love your dog. And, of course, you love your children (most of the time). Even within a relationship, there are seasons that include new love and mature love. And don't you just love having the Internet at your fingertips these days, with instant access to knowledge?

The word *love* appears throughout the Bible 310 times. More than 300 times, God's Word talks about this mighty, powerful, difficult term. First John 4:7–8 says, "Dear friends, let us love one another, for love comes from God. Everyone who loves has been born of God and knows God. Whoever does not love does not know God, because God is love."

That's right. God *is* love. So, for all the ways we use it and define it and feel it and choose it, it all comes back to the Lord. He created us to love us. And because He loves us, He sent His one and only Son to die for us (John 3:16).

Today I encourage you to rest in that. No matter where you are, what you might be dealing with, or how you might feel, you are wrapped in love by the One who made you. Because God is love, there is nothing we can do that would make us unlovable.

No matter how often I am tripped up by my quick temper, lack of forgiveness, or knack for taking control of my own circumstances, Christ envelops me in His arms and gently whispers to my spirit that He loves me and created me to do the same. No matter what, choose to love one another with an abiding love that can come only from the Father above.

How can you see God's love demonstrated in your own life? Whom can you show love to today?

Dear God, I come before You today to ask that You would reveal love to me in unexpected ways. I also ask that I would demonstrate love to those around me, and that I would receive Your love and trust its breadth for me. Lord, thank You for loving me first so that I can reflect Your love to others every day.

/ˈlīf/

noun

1. the period from birth to death
2. spiritual existence transcending physical death
3. a way or manner of living
4. a vital or living being

TWO

LIFE

◆

As water reflects the face, so one's life reflects the heart.

PROVERBS 27:19

When I painted my first angel, I had no idea the impact these ethereal beings sculpted from oil paint would have on people. As I speculate on why this might be, one thing that comes to mind is that I have met so many people who share countless stories reflecting the theme "life is short."

Recently I have had several people in my life lose friends and family members at an early age. Walking down memory lane on social media, I came across a family whose daughter had become very close to my daughters and me. This sweet girl passed away at just eight years old. Whether eight or eighty, life is always too short. And perhaps there's something in the angels that provides comfort.

Each of us has been given the gift of life, and when we are handed that gift, we are also entrusted with the responsibility to live our lives. We are given a choice how to define our days by our words and actions. Scripture tells us that we are not promised tomorrow and that each day has enough trouble of its own (Matthew 6:34).

Each of us will face challenges throughout our lives. I was talking to a friend during the middle of a challenging season, and she told me, "I don't question God about the *why*. I just ask Him to give me strength through it all." I hope to always keep this perspective in the midst of trials and not question His *why*, but rather focus on glorifying Him in all circumstances.

I certainly do not ever want to belittle or minimize the sadness or pain that accompanies loss. I do, however, want to encourage you along the way to grab hold of the God who will equip and strengthen you. Wake up each morning with your eyes fixed on Jesus and a heart filled with gratitude. Even when our days seem long, they are so short in comparison to the eternity that awaits us in the kingdom!

I'm reminded of this poignant poem:

> Life is short . . . live it.
>
> Love is rare . . . grab it.
>
> Anger is bad . . . dump it.
>
> Fear is awful . . . face it.
>
> Memories are sweet . . . cherish them.
>
> Friends are precious . . . embrace them.
>
> God is good . . . praise Him.
>
> —AUTHOR UNKNOWN

Your life is precious. Has an area of your life been feeling a little stagnant? Can you see God breathing new life in those areas that seem a little lifeless?

Dear God, thank You for exhaling Your divine breath so that I might have lungs full of oxygen. Thank You for choosing for me to have another day on this earth so that I can continue to walk in the purpose You created for me. Show me how to embrace this life fully today so I can be a walking testimony to the goodness You have woven throughout my life.

Gift

/ˈgift/

noun

1. something voluntarily transferred by one person to another without compensation; a present
2. a notable capacity, talent, or endowment

verb

1. to endow with some power, quality, or attribute
2. to voluntarily transfer something to another person without compensation; to give a present

THREE

GIFT

◆

"You are the light of the world. A town built on a hill cannot be hidden. Neither do people light a lamp and put it under a bowl. Instead they put it on its stand, and it gives light to everyone in the house. In the same way, let your light shine before others, that they may see your good deeds and glorify your Father in heaven."

MATTHEW 5:14–16

The most frequent comment I hear from people is how busy I am. Sure, I'm a wife, a mother, an artist, and a business owner, but God has called me to each of these roles. So if I'm *busy*, I'm busy being obedient to Him and using the gifts with which He has entrusted me.

When we are serving out our calling and using the gifts God has put in our lives, life doesn't feel busy. Instead, walking the path of our calling leaves us feeling enlivened and fulfilled—like we're a part of the Lord's masterful plan. "Busy" happens when we're not clear about our purpose or calling, and then allow external voices and circumstances to complicate our lives.

Amid jam-packed schedules—whether driving multiple carpools or working as a CEO, a doctor, a teacher, a mother, a volunteer—I encourage us to stop glorifying how *busy* we are. Focus instead on following your callings, however many there may be, and using your gifts to the glory of the Lord. I love using the following acronym when people comment on how "busy" I am:

BUSYBUSY

Be Uniquely Serving Yahweh By Using [what is] Specifically Yours

Each of us has been given a gift. And each of us has a role to play in the world God has created for us. If you're feeling too busy or frazzled, I challenge you to pause and evaluate what it is that fulfills you rather than being in a constant state of increased craze. Serve Him with what He has given you and find the peace and joy He has promised you!

What wonderful gifts are you offering to the world today? How has being "busy" robbed you of your unique expression? How has it robbed you of God's blessings and joy?

Dear God, thank You for granting me Your precious gifts. Thank You for calling me to be Yours and entrusting me with these gifts and abilities. Help me stop wishing for someone else's talents and instead walk confidently in my own so that I can glorify You all the days of my life.

Joy

/ˈjoi/

noun

1. the emotion evoked by well-being, success, or good for-
   tune or by the prospect of possessing what one desires;
   delight
2. a state of happiness or felicity; bliss

FOUR

JOY

◆

Splendor and majesty are before him; strength
and joy are in his dwelling place.

1 CHRONICLES 16:27

---

oy is my first name. It's also my mother's first name. However, it is a name that I ran from throughout my childhood. When I filled out my college application, I transposed my name to Anne Joy (instead of Joy Anne). Let me just say—the registrar's office wasn't too happy about that.

My kids will tell you that I lack joy. They consider me a helicopter mom—always worried, always demanding, always enforcing rules and curfews. As a result, I've been spending a lot of time with God, asking Him to fill me with pure joy. No matter my circumstances or surroundings, I want to be filled with the joy that comes only from the Lord—a joy that no one and nothing can steal.

Happiness is conditional on circumstances—what I'm wearing, how my nails look, if I'm having a good hair day, if I sell a piece of my art. Happiness shows up, and then it vanishes because of other circumstances—a costly car repair, a tense conversation, something not going my way. That's the problem with "being happy." It's elusive, a temporary state. Happiness "happens," and it ebbs and flows.

Joy, on the other hand, lasts. Joy isn't influenced by the circumstances swirling around me. Joy is rooted in trusting the identity of who I am in Christ and how He sees me. I am joyful because I am His. God's fierce love equals joy. I am learning how to laugh with my kids (it's okay that they still think I am a helicopter mom most of the time), and I am finding times to crack a joke or two.

There are so many threats to our joy: the lies of the enemy, doubt, fear, anxiety, bad news from the doctor, the loss of a dear friend. Recently I lost my best high school friend, who had battled cancer. But as two hundred guests gathered, all dressed in white to celebrate her life, there amid the grief and mourning were joy and rejoicing. We must wake up each day and claim joy—choosing to acknowledge the joy that already exists because God allowed us to see a new day and an opportunity to live for Him.

This year we will experience moments of exhilaration, triumph, victory—and, yes, happiness—but also, surely, moments of sadness, grief, and struggle. Thanks to the seeds the Lord has planted in us, we can choose joy to amplify His goodness despite our trials.

What good and perfect gifts has God given you that remind you to choose joy? What brings you the most joy in the face of life's struggles?

Dear God, You are the fullness of joy, and because I am Your child, I know that joy resides in me. Today I ask that You reveal Yourself through unexpected joys. Help me stop chasing temporary happiness and instead find unending delight in Your joy.

Obedience

/ō-ˈbē-dē-ən(t)s/

noun

1. an act or instance of obeying
2. a sphere of jurisdiction, especially an ecclesiastical or sometimes secular dominion

FIVE

OBEDIENCE

◆

Do not merely listen to the word, and so deceive yourselves.
Do what it says.

JAMES 1:22

When my kids were little, I taught an Art & Soul class once a week to all their friends. My house would be flooded in the afternoons with elementary-age kids. Our sessions consisted of an hour-long Bible lesson followed by an art project.

One lesson I loved to teach was about the condition of our hearts. I had a beautiful bowl hand-painted on both the interior and exterior. I explained to the children about the condition of our hearts, and how God was a holy God and could not be in the presence of sin. We would then discuss things that would disappoint God. They would call out things such as lying, cheating, and fighting. I would write each word on a separate slip of paper, wad up the paper, and put it in the bowl.

It didn't take long before the pieces of paper were covering the beauty inside the bowl. We would examine it together and talk about the condition of our hearts with all of this "junk" inside. Then we memorized Psalm 51:10 and prayed that God would give us clean hearts. I explained that all we needed to do was be obedient each day and dump out our own "junk" before God each night, as I physically dumped out our bowl of paper into a trash can.

As an adult, I have found that the "junk" isn't always as simplistic as those children described. Years of resentment, harboring anger, furthering generational sin patterns all create clutter in our hearts, but God can handle the complexities of life. The process is the same for us as it was for my Art & Soul students. As we lay our mess before His throne, He will do the heavy lifting to clean our hearts—but *we* have to do it out of obedience every day. His mercies are new each and every morning.

Examine the condition of your heart today. Where have you gathered unnecessary clutter? Pray and identify the "junk" that is piled up in your heart. Maybe it has been accumulating into a giant, overflowing heap for years, or maybe it simply piles up a little each day. Whatever the case may be, you are hiding the beauty God painted within your heart. Ask Him to remove it as often as you can. Ask that He would rebuild, renew, and fortify your spirit and purify your heart daily.

Dear God, my ask isn't a fun one today, but I invite You here with me to reveal the "junk" in my life that is weighing me down and distracting me from fellowship with You. I ask You to partner with me to remove it so that I may be renewed.

/ˈwiz-dəm/

noun

1. the ability to discern inner qualities and relationships; insight
2. good sense; judgment

SIX

WISDOM

---◆---

But the wisdom that comes from heaven is first of all
pure; then peace-loving, considerate, submissive, full of
mercy and good fruit, impartial and sincere.

JAMES 3:17

As I age, my appearance ages as well. As my hair shows more and more signs of the years I've lived, I hope to embrace it as a token of what God has brought me through in this life—every peak and every valley, equally.

Surely you have those confidants whose advice you seek, whose spirit is attractive, oozing wisdom and wise counsel. I know I do. And I can't help but think of how the Lord richly rewarded Solomon, who was able to request any gift from Him, and he asked for God's wisdom.

Just like Solomon, we have the power to request *any* gift from the Lord, yet how often do we ask for His wisdom? His will, yes. His direction, sure. But His rich, all-consuming wisdom? Not as often.

We innately and naturally value wisdom in our relationships, and we know (with each new gray hair that sprouts up) that we are acquiring new wisdom as we face and overcome the many trials we encounter. And what a mighty follower we would have to be to come face-to-face with our Creator and ask Him to give us a slice of His wisdom.

I love the way Scripture weaves together a narrative. Proverbs 31 tells us that beauty is fleeting, but the fear of the Lord is to be praised. Proverbs 9 says the fear of the Lord is the beginning of wisdom. Maybe it's no surprise then that as our youthful looks fade, our wisdom increases. In fact, I'm choosing to believe that as I gain wisdom, and as I seek God to receive it, the grays I'm gaining are even more beautiful, showcasing that I'm drawing nearer to Him.

Wisdom is beautiful, and it pleases God's heart for you to dive deeper to obtain it.

What does wisdom look like to you? Who are the wise people around you? Is there something you're struggling with that you could share in order to gain wise access around the subject? Don't be afraid to ask! Use this as a divine opportunity for those wise people to use the gift of wisdom to serve.

Dear God, thank You for the opportunity to experience true wisdom. Thank You for being a good and gracious Father who imparts Your wisdom to me. I want to know more and experience more with You. Today I ask You to share new wisdom with me so that I may learn even more about You.

Habit

/'ha-bət/

noun

1. a settled tendency or usual manner of behavior
2. an acquired mode of behavior that has become nearly or completely involuntary

SEVEN

HABIT

---◆---

I can do all things through him who strengthens me.
PHILIPPIANS 4:13 ESV

---

ately I've spent time talking to friends and employees about how to achieve a work-life balance, how to wear multiple hats well, and how to keep focus and priorities aligned with the Lord. It's easy to talk about, but difficult to do. The foundation, for me, undoubtedly lies in the Word of God.

I carve out quiet time each morning to absorb God's truth. Those moments become my rudder and set the direction for my day. Later, when I feel like I'm dog-paddling amid chaos, this gives my heart and mind something sound to reflect on. Having quality time with God must be what a weary traveler experiences when he or she stumbles upon an oasis in a desert: refreshment, renewal, and cleansing.

I've established other habits that help my heart focus on the Lord. Throughout the day, particularly when I'm painting, I keep praise and worship music playing. The powerful words streaming into my ears and heart reinforce God's promises.

Another habit is journaling—actively writing and practicing the elements of Scripture and creating a living dialogue between me and the Lord. This helps reinforce the depth of His words in my own life. By journaling, we can revisit the trials He has led us through and how His hand helped us along the journey. I'm reminded over and over again that with each trial comes great learning and wisdom, and I can see victories both large and small along the way.

Another habit is setting an alarm on my phone with favorite Scriptures fully written out in the phone calendar. I have several, but one of my favorites is Ephesians 3:20, which repeats daily and pops up on my phone at 3:20 p.m. to remind me that God can do immeasurably more than we could ever ask or imagine. When that alarm sounds, and God's Word appears, I meditate on the scripture at hand and am reminded of God's Word and His hand on my life and circumstances. Setting these habits steers the direction of my heart throughout the day.

If you're just beginning to establish daily Christ-centered habits, I encourage you to begin by digging into the Word for a few minutes each day. Choose a verse and write it on your heart. Memorize it. Repeat it. Write it down. Have the scripture pop up on your phone every day. Claim it as your own mantra or battle cry. This simple step will have an impact on the course of your day and guide you into the weeks ahead. It will give you strength for whatever you are facing in life.

It's all too easy to pick up poor habits that draw our focus away from the Lord. What habits do you feel called to create for yourself? What Christ-centered habit can you begin today?

Dear God, it has become all too easy to find myself entangled in bad habits, but I know that my love for You will grow as I seek You daily. God, thank You for Your patience with me when I get distracted. Please embolden me to shed the negative habits that are keeping me burdened and away from You.

Guide

/ˈgīd/

noun

1. one who leads or directs another's way
2. a person who directs another's conduct or course of life

EIGHT

GUIDE

◆

"My sheep listen to my voice; I know them, and they follow me."

JOHN 10:27

Recently I've been flying a lot. A fun and poignant mixture of visiting my girls in college, comforting grieving friends, attending speaking engagements, and just traveling for fun has me up in the clouds, and it's given me time to think about how unnatural flight really is. If you think about it, it takes a whole lot of faith to climb aboard a huge aircraft and trust that the enormous, heavy bird composed of metal and bolts will carry you to your destination.

On some flights, the captain will announce, "This is your captain speaking," followed by a reassuring monologue about the expected ease or bumpiness of the upcoming flight, the altitude to which we will be climbing, and the weather conditions we will encounter. I like these flights. I like hearing the voice of the person in control of the aircraft.

On other flights, the pilots don't say a word. You are sitting on the tarmac for what seems like hours and . . . nothing. Not a word. No echoing voices from the cockpit. Instead, I scan the faces of the flight attendants instructing us about safety measures and exit rows and beverage options and wonder, *Who's in charge here?*

In the same way those tons of steel and screws defy gravity and shouldn't logistically be able to fly long distances, there's no logical reason my own baggage and burdens should have brought me to where I am in my life now. Whether I'm experiencing the turbulence that comes from mothering teenagers and adult children, or clear skies while worshiping and painting in my studio, I can hear God's voice say, "This is your Father speaking, and I'm in control."

Flying through life without seeking God's reassuring voice seems reckless and confusing. Where do you seek peace when the turbulence hits? Whom do you turn to for guidance? For me, the answer is easy. I open my Bible. Page after page, God's Word gives me guidance, affirmation, confidence, and restored faith. I hear my Father's voice—the Captain of my life—echoing, "Don't worry; I am in control."

I am so appreciative there are no guarantees that my walk with the Lord will be flawless or easy or without turbulence, but I can rest assured that my Pilot, my Captain, is the perfect guide.

How is God guiding you today? Where and how is He leading you?

Dear God, thank You for Your divine guidance. Thank You for steering me safely through choppy waters and gently leading me across smooth seas to solid ground. Lord, I ask that when I feel trials and tribulations around me, I would not be shaken, but that I would find peace because You are my constant Guide.

Surrender

/sə-ˈren-dər/

verb

1. to yield to the power, control, or possession of another upon compulsion or demand
2. to give oneself up into the power of another; to yield

NINE

SURRENDER

Surrender your heart to God, turn to him in prayer, and
give up your sins—even those you do in secret. Then you
won't be ashamed; you will be confident and fearless.

JOB 11:13–15 CEV

everal Christmases ago challenged my spirit. With five adults and one almost-adult under one roof, tensions ran high, and I found myself losing my joy among kids bickering, too many to-dos, not enough time, and a calendar full of obligations. I was operating from an empty emotional fuel tank and feeling the effects of burnout.

Several days after Christmas, my family and I were hosting a party for some of our closest friends and neighbors. When the team arrived to assemble a tent in our backyard, they did so during a deluge. Our town of Charlotte, North Carolina, had been experiencing what can only be described as "the days of Noah" for weeks, with even more rain in the forecast.

Admittedly, I became frazzled. I walked outside, under the tent, to reflect on the events of the recent holiday, along with my emotions during the past several days, including my disappointment with the soggy ground I was walking on. As I stood under the tent, something inside me broke. Amid the storm, I finally let my heart listen closely to what God was saying, and I heard the still, small whisper, "Just surrender to Me, Anne."

I sobbed uncontrollably and spent time under that tent repenting for spending Christmas so focused on tasks while completely missing the meaning and ultimately stripping away the joy—for myself and for others. When I rush from thing to thing to thing, I position myself as pacesetter, a goal achiever, a life planner instead of submitting that role to God. I need time and frequent reminders to place myself back where I belong—in submission to the Lord—to reposition myself into a posture of surrender.

As each new season brings its own challenges, my constant prayer and focus will be for my own surrender. Personally, I want to maintain that posture of surrender at the feet of the Lord to guide my home, my faith, my family, my work, and my marriage. And for my business, our team is prayerfully surrendering to the plans God has for me. Only by surrendering to Him and shedding our own plans and pride can we walk the path that God has planned for us.

What is God tugging at your heart right now to surrender? As you let go and let God into the many places you have surrendered, I pray you would feel His presence and His peace that passes all understanding.

Dear God, today I surrender, releasing my pride, my sin, and my plans, and I fall at Your feet in surrender. I know that sharing with You all the secret, ugly things I've been hiding will provide a new, confident stride in my step. Thank You for accepting me just as I am.

Foundation

/faὑn-ˈdā-shən/

noun

1. a basis, such as a tenet, principle, or axiom, upon which something stands or is supported
2. an underlying base or support
3. a body or ground upon which something is built up or overlaid

TEN

FOUNDATION

◆

So this is what the Sovereign LORD says: "See, I lay a stone in Zion, a tested stone, a precious cornerstone for a sure foundation; the one who relies on it will never be stricken with panic."

ISAIAH 28:16

Laying a foundation is vital to structural integrity, and digging is an essential process of building faith.

Have you ever watched babies try to walk for the first time? Their feet are disproportionately small, and their steps are uncertain and nearly drunken. More often than not, their first steps end up in a face-plant and a goose egg. They have a shaky foundation.

Foundations aren't glamorous. Home and lifestyle magazines rarely highlight the artisanship of a home's foundation, but I assure you, the masterful design is there. To lay a foundation, builders must dig. Even in work as delicate as gardening, a seed cannot be planted or sprout without the gardener first digging out ground to nestle the seed in the dirt, planting its foundation.

We built our home more than seventeen years ago. I remember showing up during the digging process for the foundation to be laid. On-site, we received the bad news that one side of the land had "bad dirt" and that the construction workers would have to dig another ten feet deeper. However, our builder had ordered "just enough" concrete for the usual foundation depth of two feet. As the day turned into night, the crew finished up the job, and we had just enough concrete—even with the gaping holes on the side of our foundation.

As I walked away, I felt Jesus tugging at my heart with a message that to have a strong spiritual foundation, we have to dig up all the "bad dirt" in our lives and hand it over to Him. When we invite Jesus to oversee the dirty work, real progress can be made to clear out the debris.

Twice in Isaiah, God is described as being a cornerstone and a sure foundation. "A tested stone, a precious cornerstone" (28:16), and "a rich store of salvation and wisdom and knowledge" (33:6). The craftsmanship and intricate design work that can take place when there is no doubt in the solidity of a strong foundation is endless, and the Lord delights in creating and designing and adorning His children with His master handiwork.

I have had a lot of "bad dirt" to dig up and clear out in my life throughout these fifty-something years. My prayer is that we neither fear nor hide the dirt in our lives. That we not shy away from the digging process, but rather allow the Lord to do the work and lay a solid foundation of His grace and mercy.

Are there any cracks in your foundation? Is your cornerstone being tested? What needs to be dug up and cleared out that you could ask God's hand in?

Dear God, You have constructed a firm foundation for me. I know that You have laid the groundwork for beauty and joy throughout my life. Today I implore You to help me feel that solid footing wherever my path leads me.

Still

/ˈstil/

adjective

1. devoid of or abstaining from motion

2. uttering no sound; quiet, subdued, muted

3. free from noise or turbulence; calm, tranquil

ELEVEN

STILL

---◆---

The LORD will fight for you, and you have only to be silent.

EXODUS 14:14 ESV

I love traveling to New York City.

Well . . . I love traveling to New York City *for a few days at a time*. After that, I need to come home. The noise gets to me—the traffic, the construction, the honking, the people—constant noise that gets inside my head and drowns out everything else. Noise can cloud your judgment, distort your thoughts, and crowd out decisions.

Even while all alone, you can be surrounded by noise, with droning television shows, incoming texts, a crowded email in-box, a head full of toxic internal dialogue. It may seem impossible to just be quiet, but multiple times in the Bible, the Lord asks us to be still and quiet.

Thomas à Kempis powerfully stated, "Blessed are the ears that hear the pulse of the divine whisperer and give no heed to the many whisperings of the world." How convicting! How many times have I missed the quiet nudging and promptings of the Holy Spirit because the world's noise rang more loudly in my ears?

God doesn't need to scream the loudest, because His Word is the most powerful. He doesn't need to shout and demand and stomp because He *is*. He is everything. There isn't anything in the cosmos that speaks louder than His gentle voice.

The women on my team were joking that their bathroom showers are their most spiritual places because they're the only quiet place in their houses. I encourage you to check the noise levels in your life. Find that quiet space—wherever it may be, both literally and figuratively. Remove yourself from the clanging ruckus that the world thrives on, and focus on the stillness and the quiet. There you will find His pulse and His voice cutting through the static and overcoming the noise.

When was the last time you were still? I invite you to take a moment to close your eyes and be still. Be silent. Notice God's presence all around you.

Dear God, my life is full of too much noise and too much chaos and too much busyness. I am consumed by the things that are competing for my attention. Thank You for Your still, small voice that cuts through the noise directly to my heart. Today help me find the space to be still and silent before You so that I can rest in the peace You provide.

Fellowship

/ˈfe-lō-ˌship/

noun

1. companionship; company
2. a company of equals or friends

TWELVE

FELLOWSHIP

◆

What is the outcome then, brethren? When you assemble, each one has a psalm, has a teaching, has a revelation, has a tongue, has an interpretation. Let all things be done for edification.

1 CORINTHIANS 14:26 NASB

I can get lost in Instagram stories for hours on end. This live feed of my friends and acquaintances lives right at my fingertips. I love the connections that social media allows us, yet I can't help but think that the ease of connection is also hurting our real, true, personal relationships with each other.

Proverbs 27:17 says, "As iron sharpens iron, so one person sharpens another." Scripture doesn't say, "As Twitter sharpens Twitter . . ." or "As Facebook sharpens Facebook . . ." No. It speaks of metal sharpening metal, which happens only when it comes into *direct* contact with another piece of metal.

Sharpening each other happens in person—in direct fellowship—in conversations, in small groups, in meals at the same table. I love the entertainment of social media, but I never want to take for granted the true identities of those people behind the accounts. I want to be increasingly intentional about the relationships I'm building.

Recently I met a friend for coffee. We had run into each other at a restaurant and said how much we'd like to get together to catch up. I reminded her (and myself) that it's never about being too busy; it's about taking the time to put it on the calendar. We scheduled a date right then, and when the morning came where we met, it was so lovely and refreshing for us both.

The New Testament word for "fellowship" is *koinonia*, which means "to come together for mutual benefit." The Lord built us for creating community with one another. He hand selected each one of us to be sitting in the unique position we are now, surrounded by the people in our lives, and no amount of filters and shares will validate or steal that. My joy is my responsibility and my treasure to protect. I dress for an audience of One and am striving for real community with the divine appointments He arranges for me.

I encourage you to set aside time for the people with whom God has entrusted you. People who are mutually beneficial to you, with whom you can be unfiltered and with whom you can share how God is working in your life.

Dear God, thank You for people. Thank You for the billions of people You have created who represent opportunities for fellowship. Thank You for the many opportunities for me to find support and encouragement and earthly glimpses of Your relational nature through those around me. Strengthen my relationships, and help me be a true friend to those around me so we can share in our faith together.

Hope

/ˈhōp/

noun

1. a desire accompanied by expectation of or belief in
   fulfillment

verb

1. to cherish a desire with anticipation; to want something
   to happen or be true
2. to expect with confidence; trust

THIRTEEN

HOPE

◆

This hope is a strong and trustworthy anchor for our souls.
It leads us through the curtain into God's inner sanctuary.

HEBREWS 6:19 NLT

My husband, Clark, and I had the wonderful privilege of taking a group of high school students to the British Virgin Islands for their senior spring break several years ago. It was one of those trips of a lifetime: breathtaking scenery, a respite from technology, and a sensation of peace that passes all understanding.

During our trip, I had a unique opportunity to talk with these kids about their futures. They were all standing on the threshold of their last summer as children before walking through the doorway to their next season into adulthood. We spent time talking about what it is that anchors them, as our own boats were tied to a buoy or anchored out in a cove.

I told them that without an anchor of faith, they would drift and be cast about by the storms and waves that come with life. Their surest anchor is in the hope provided by a God who loves them no matter which way the tides ebb and flow. The Creator who paints each wave and commands the seas to calm also provides Himself to us as an anchor to grasp in the midst of choppy waters.

The beauty of having a boat equipped with an anchor is that we were able not only to travel from excursion to excursion, but to do so without worry of passing the spot where we needed to stop to actually enjoy our time. An anchor didn't hold us back. It allowed us to experience our time to the fullest. An anchoring faith, in the same way, won't hold your life back, but rather it will provide the freedom to move hopefully from season to season without fear of casually drifting by your port of call.

In between bouts of laughter so deep that our sides hurt and intimate moments of life-giving truths, I watched these precious young souls bask in the sunshine and prepare themselves for a future that will assuredly carry its fair days of clouds. My prayer is that they—and you—would know that there is a God who loves us. That He has a plan. We are not simply flotsam and jetsam, randomly battered about by the seas of our lives.

What secret hopes have you been afraid to share with God? He already knows your heart; He's just waiting for you to ask.

Dear God, thank You for the anchor of hope. Thank You that even when I face the insurmountable, I have a true constant in hope. Without that, God, I would feel adrift, but the gift of hope always draws me back to You. Help me find hope even when it feels like it is missing. Help me feel the pull of that anchor securing me to You.

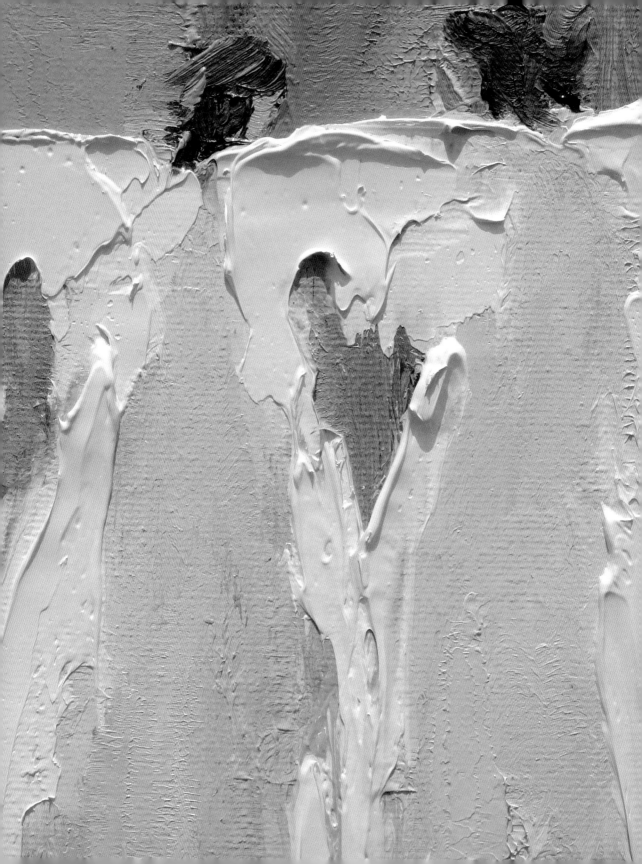

Connect

/kə-ˈnekt/

verb

1. to become joined
2. to have or establish a rapport

FOURTEEN

CONNECT

---◆---

Then you will call upon Me and go and pray
to Me, and I will listen to you.
JEREMIAH 29:12 NKJV

---

onnection is a popular topic. These days we are so connected to each other—with just a push or swipe, in an instant. In fact, most of us are equipped with multiple devices that can connect us to one another no matter where on the planet we are.

Heck, two of my four kids took the most amazing trip halfway around the world, and still, every day, we connected via FaceTime. Through my screen I could see their surroundings. I could see exactly where they were, the beauty of each place they went—*instantly*. Their time zone had them half a day ahead of me, so basically, I was seeing the future.

My daughter FaceTimed me during times of concern and times of pure bliss. Even thinking about it now, I can recall so well how excited I was to get that video call each and every day.

This reminds me of our God. You know the One. The God who created us for connection. He made Adam and Eve to fellowship with Him and also with each other. We were literally made for the pure joy of relationship. With that in mind, can you even imagine how excited He would be if we connected to Him *every* day. What would that look like?

Look—I'm human. There are days that I wake up and snuggle in my chair, open my Bible, journal, and pray. And then there are the days that I wake up and fly out the door, rushed and in a hurry. The days that I can linger and really dig deeper into God's Word without distraction, being still and sitting in silence while worshiping, are truly the most precious times of connection with our living, breathing Creator. These are the times that fuel my soul and sustain me. There is a noticeable difference in my quality of life on those days. I'm rested and recharged instead of frazzled and overwhelmed.

Can you take a moment today to connect with your Creator? Pray or meditate to connect and cultivate your relationship with God and notice how He tries to connect with you throughout your day. And notice the enhanced quality of your day as a result.

Dear God, today You connected with me. Yesterday You did the same. And all the days before and ahead of me, You have made connections directly to me and for me. Thank You for always being accessible to me so that I may rest, recharge, and reset.

Create

/krē-ˈāt/

verb

1. to bring into existence
2. to produce or bring about by a course of action or behavior
3. to produce through imaginative skill; design

FIFTEEN

CREATE

◆

He has filled them with skill to do all kinds of work as engravers,
designers, embroiderers in blue, purple, and scarlet yarn and fine
linen, and weavers—all of them skilled workers and designers.

EXODUS 35:35

When I was a little girl, I was always creating something, whether it was handmade pocketbooks or a papier-mâché piggy bank or writing. I had a wild imagination, and I knew that one day I would do something with art or books. I spent hours doodling. In third grade, I penned an essay that began, "When I grow up, I'm going to be an artist." This essay gave me the chance to flex my dreaming muscles about my art career.

To this day, I love hearing the dreams planted in young children's hearts. Pablo Picasso famously said, "Every child is an artist. The problem is how to remain an artist when we grow up."

Fast-forward to my high school years, when I received a D in my studio art class. Friends, I very nearly failed my dream. I wasn't the most academic, but *surely* I would excel in *this* part of my dream, right?

Sometimes in my studio I'll approach my canvas with a vision of an angel with spread wings and empty hands, only to find through the process of painting and being led by worship music that what appears instead is an angel with folded wings and a violin, perched to praise the Lord. Different from my original vision, but these detours include details He uses to encourage just the right person, for reasons I may not comprehend in the moment.

Back in art class, however, I didn't have that foundation of faith. Instead, I allowed doubt to creep into my heart as I wondered if maybe I'd misunderstood God. In fact, I took my *own* detour, studying elementary education. Later, I taught third grade, and for those years, my heart and hands were full, shepherding precious children and encouraging them to follow their wild hopes and unfiltered dreams.

Our God is the ultimate Creator, and He instilled in each of us our own creative expression. I simply submit myself to the process, knowing that grades, rankings, and reviews don't define me. I can stand with confidence, knowing full well that the Creator's vision for my life far exceeds any human opinion.

God made each of us in His image, and since He is the greatest creator, we have access to that same creativity. How do you express creativity? In meals you cook? Through fashion? Architecture or engineering? How can you use God's confidence to cultivate your creative expression to share with the world?

Dear God, thank You for creating me. Thank You for instilling within my heart the desire and ability to create. Remind me today, Lord, that when I create beauty, it's because of You, and when I create messes, You can fix them. Thank You for Your artistry, Lord, that gives me so many reminders of Your splendor each day.

/ˈwit-nəs/

noun

1. attestation of a fact or event; testimony
2. one who gives evidence
3. one who has personal knowledge of something

SIXTEEN

WITNESS

─────────◆─────────

How beautiful are the feet of those who bring good news!

ROMANS 10:15

─────────────────────

don't know if you're somebody who swears by personality assessments, whether it's by way of a Myers-Briggs personality inventory, an Enneagram type description, or simple quizzes found in magazines. The thing I *do* know is that each of us has a different personality.

My best friend can sit on a plane next to a complete stranger and strike up a conversation in a hot second and within five minutes of takeoff knows that person's life story. In fact, by then she has also witnessed to them about a living Jesus who is there for them in any situation and she will waltz off the plane with a new friend.

As for me . . . well . . . not so much. I do not strike up conversations on an airplane. I immediately radiate the antisocial vibes, and if my forehead had a neon sign, it would flash, "I do not want to talk. Do not disturb." At times I feel guilty that I am not always willing to open up and witness to others, but I am also reminded that we each have been given our own personality, and as part of that, God has given each of us our own spiritual gifts to match.

Rather than wishing I had my best friend's gifting, or the gifts I see displayed in someone on social media, it's my command to seek the Lord about what He has given to me. When we are walking close with Him, our actions become our witness.

I love the quote, "Preach the gospel at all times. Use words if necessary." In today's world, when it feels as though we're surrounded by darkness and discontent, we can all grow in our ability to be a witness of the gospel, to be that light that shines, and to be bearers of good news. While I'm not great at doing this on an airplane (yet), I know that whenever someone steps into my gallery or studio, I am excited and lit up, ready to share all that God has done in my life.

So, if you're a talker, *talk*! Share the good news of what God is doing in your life and what He has brought you through. If you are the quiet type, that's fine! Witness to others through your actions—maybe the way you offer a gentle smile at the grocery checkout or a simple wave to a neighbor.

Whatever your gift, and whatever your personality, how can you be a witness for the kingdom just as you are?

Dear God, I ask that You empower me to be a witness for You. Please free me from the insecurity or fear that too often keeps me quiet. Instead, I invite You to place Your divine appointments in my path, and I ask that You would cause me to be bold the next time I have the opportunity to share about You.

Worship

/ˈwər-shəp/

noun

1. reverence offered a divine being or supernatural power
2. a form of religious practice with its creed and ritual

verb

1. to honor or show reverence for as a divine being or supernatural power
2. to regard with a great or extravagant respect, honor, or devotion

SEVENTEEN

WORSHIP

---- ◆ ----

"Worthy are you, our Lord and God, to receive glory
and honor and power, for you created all things, and
by your will they existed and were created."

REVELATION 4:11 ESV

When you hear the word *worship*, what does it trigger in your heart? It's a big word, and it's paired with big responsibility. Put simply, worship is not just about going to church one day a week—even if you go every week—or singing songs during the service.

Before we worship a holy God, our hearts have to be positioned in the right posture, pure and clean. We have to come before our righteous God and ask that He would cleanse us of all our iniquities. For me, this is daily, and wow, do I have many—including worry, fear, control, distraction, and much more. After the cleansing of our hearts begins, the ultimate worship can overtake our souls.

In Romans 12:1, the Greek word for "worship" is *latreia*, which means "divine service and adoration of God."

Have you ever thought of all the ways we can express our adoration to God? We can worship through music, prayer, praise, and thanksgiving; through reading the Word; through giving; through serving; through confession of sin; and through spending time in nature, appreciating His creation. Whether you are standing with your hands raised or bowing down in supplication on your bedroom floor, clapping or dancing, running on a treadmill, seated in a cozy chair, standing on a crowded subway—in silence or chaos—you can worship Him and thank Him for all He is doing in your life.

For me, my favorite way is worshiping through music, especially listening in my studio while painting. During these holy times, I let the words of the worship music sink deep into my soul as I praise our faithful God, whose ultimate desire is to connect with you and me.

Scripture says, "Give to the Lord the glory he deserves!" (Psalm 96:8 NLT). The promise is that when we worship God in this way, He will come and commune with us, and will respond to our worship by making our hearts more like His.

No matter what or where or how, I invite you to ponder and reflect on this word today and how you are worshiping Him. Discover this beautiful gift and the way it enhances your relationship with God.

Dear God, today I worship You. I don't ask anything of You today, but instead I want to spend time thanking You for Your perfection. You are sovereign and wise and present and loving. Thank You for giving me so many ways to worship You—through music, my work, my home, and my prayers. You are a good God, and I love You.

Gratitude

/ˈgra-tə-ˌtüd/

noun

1. the state of being grateful; thankfulness

Rest

/ˈrest/

noun

1. repose; sleep
2. freedom from activity or labor
3. peace of mind or spirit

NINETEEN

REST

---◆---

"Come to me, all you who are weary and
burdened, and I will give you rest."

MATTHEW 11:28 NLT

ebster's definition of the word *rest* is "relief or freedom, especially from anything that wearies, troubles or disturbs." Whew. Do you have anything that wearies you? Troubles you? Disturbs you? Don't we all?

In all our troubles, whether big or small, we must remember all that God has done throughout His Word. He delivered Moses and the Israelites from slavery, and even when they wandered for forty years, He was speaking promises over them about the new life they were about to enter. Even through seasons of barrenness, He was whispering promises to Hannah about her child to come.

We cannot deny the pains we are in now, or those we might go through, or even what we have been through. The beauty of being a believer, however, is that we can remember God's faithfulness and give thanks as we trust in His mercy.

At that point, we're able to rest in Him. I believe the ultimate rest is found in the center of Christ. And how we find that holy center is by relying on Him unconditionally. Barrenness? Remember Hannah's prayer in Samuel.

Persecution? Remember Paul's deliverance from prison in Acts. The stories go on and on.

As we let the light of Christ shine through us, we are increasingly able to surrender all our hopes and fears and desires to a living Lord who loves us more than anything in this world. We thank Him every minute of the day for every trial and for every blessing. At that intersection, we will find rest.

Rely.

Engage.

Surrender.

Trust.

Where can you find rest today?

Dear God, thank You for taking the things out of my hands that feel too heavy. Thank You for promising that I don't have to bear any burdens on my own. Thank You, God, for giving me a sanctuary and refuge when the world is too hard. Thank You for providing me rest.

/ə-ˈshu̇r-ən(t)s/

noun

1. a being certain in the mind
2. confidence of mind or manner; easy freedom from self-doubt or uncertainty

TWENTY

ASSURANCE

Let us draw near with a sincere heart and with the full assurance
that faith brings, having our hearts sprinkled to cleanse us from a
guilty conscience and having our bodies washed with pure water.

HEBREWS 10:22

Few things can be classified as timeless: A little black dress. A work of art. Classical music. Certainly not the pop culture icons swarming my news feed these days.

Our family dynamics are experiencing change. Our home, once bustling with toddler voices, has now dwindled in volume as my last child has left the nest. My hobby of painting in my home studio years ago has transformed into an incredible full-time business and ministry that continues to grow.

As I take inventory of these changes swirling around me, I'm reminded that we serve a God who never changes. He is constant. Daily, I have to cling to His word in Isaiah that His commands are timeless and "stand forever" (Isaiah 40:8 ESV).

Not only is His Word true, it's everlasting. In Ecclesiastes 3, Solomon makes mention of there being a season for everything under the sun—everything except for the One who created that very sun.

No matter what changes you are facing—the joy of adding a new life to your family, or the heartache of being unable to; the wonder of a new marriage, or the devastation of a crumbling one; the relief of good health, or the anxiety of a questionable report—you can rest with full assurance knowing that the One who holds you in the palm of His hand is the One who will not change.

I pray that regardless of circumstances, we will cling to a God who assures us He will never forsake us. Let us not fear imbalance, instability, or change, but let us instead anchor ourselves with the knowledge that He is good, He is true, and His love is steadfast and unwavering.

What changes are happening in your life? How are you adjusting to them? Are you fighting God or submitting to Him?

Dear God, help me not be afraid of the things that are coming my way. Few things are certain these days, but Your abiding love is one of them. Your peace that surpasses all understanding is one of them. Thank You for gentle reminders of Your steadfastness day after day.

Abundance

/ə-ˈbən-dən(t)s/

noun

1. an ample quantity
2. affluence; wealth
3. relative degree of plentifulness

TWENTY-ONE

ABUNDANCE

"I came that they may have life and have it abundantly."

JOHN 10:10 ESV

In Luke 5:5–7, Simon says to Jesus, "'Master, we've worked hard all night and haven't caught anything. But because you say so, I will let down the nets.' When they had done so, they caught such a large number of fish that their nets began to break. So they signaled their partners in the other boat to come and help them, and they came and filled both boats so full that they began to sink."

The disciples were weary. They had fished all night, battling choppy waves and empty nets. Any mom probably has immediate flashbacks to those first nights (or months, if we're being honest) after bringing a newborn home from the hospital. You were weary. You worked all night! And mothers of teenagers, you know those early helpless days come back anew, and your nights are full of waking hours of prayer and anxiety.

Jesus casually throws out the suggestion, "Hey, guys! Why don't you just switch sides?" And suddenly they had a new problem on their hands. They weren't battling empty nets anymore; they were wrestling nets so full they were breaking! The Lord answered their despondent cries, yet the disciples were unprepared to handle the abundant provision flooding in. Their physical needs were begging, but their hearts weren't ready for the answer.

I always prayed for a large family. Without my four children, my nets would feel unbearably empty. But in the midst of parenting a family of teenagers and young adults, my nets felt like they were breaking some days. No matter what, I need to apply the same diligence that identifies the emptiness of my nets to preparations for His promised abundance.

I am thankful that the Lord who provides the nets will stock my supply. He has called me to fish, and His pond is full and deep. Whether you're a teacher shepherding a classroom, a new employee praying for influence in your workplace, a stay-at-home mother trying to steward your flock, or an empty nester redefining your home, the Lord promises provision if you simply cast your nets in His waters.

What nets are you asking God to fill today? How are you preparing for the abundance that Scripture promises?

Dear God, You know the areas of my life that feel like empty nets. Thank You for Your reminder in Scripture that You won't leave my nets that way. I ask that You show me a new way to fish so that I experience Your abundance in its entirety. I ask that I never feel depleted but rather see my wants as opportunities to experience You in a new way.

Strength

/ˈstreŋ(k)th/

noun

1. the quality or state of being strong; capacity for exertion or endurance
2. the power to resist force
3. the property of being in accord with fact or reality

TWENTY-TWO

STRENGTH

◆

So do not fear, for I am with you; do not be dismayed,
for I am your God. I will strengthen you and help you;
I will uphold you with my righteous right hand.

ISAIAH 41:10

One of my favorite activities at the beach is riding bikes on a wide, firm coastline. During one incredibly beautiful day, my husband and I set out pedaling on such a beach. The sky was a brilliant blue, the sand was firm and easy to coast across, and the wind was behind us, propelling us forward.

But then it was time to turn around, and we were faced with the struggle of riding against the wind. Each pedal stroke felt like it required all of my strength, concentration, and energy. Despite how strong I thought I was, I was simply exhausting myself against the wind and not making the progress I had hoped.

Above the whipping gale, I heard a gentle whisper to my heart. God was reminding me that when I try to do things in my own strength, the struggle will always be present. When I surrender to Him and the power of His Holy Spirit, I may be exerting effort and energy, but I have the strength of the wind pushing me forward.

The beauty of a daily walk with Christ is that at any time, when the winds of the world become too overwhelming and the firm coastline turns into shifting quicksand, all I need to do is turn around. And every time I turn, there He is. His embrace and His comforting touch are a gentle, balmy breeze in the face of worldly gusts. His promises and His Word are firm and solid ground.

I'm thankful for a God whose strength and truths accompany me on life's seemingly mundane adventures. The Lord's assurance speaks through His very creation and constantly points to the Creator, who is beckoning us to turn around and let His wind be at our backs, His strength be our foundation.

As you look ahead to your day or week, where could you use God's strength? In what situations do you find yourself feeling weak? Where can God come alongside and offer His mighty protection?

Dear God, in today's world I don't know whom to trust. I don't know where to find sources I can rely on. But You have gifted me with Your Word and strength to steer me and guide my paths without fail. Thank You for those verses that provide clear passage from season to season.

Provision

/prə-ˈvi-zhən/

noun

1. the act or process of providing

2. the fact or state of being prepared beforehand

3. a stock of needed materials or supplies

TWENTY-THREE

PROVISION

◆

I will bless her with abundant provisions; her poor I will satisfy with food.

Psalm 132:15

God loves showing off His provision to us even in the smallest of details. For me, I find myself praising Him and giving Him glory when I find a prime parking spot. My God cares about my life, and He takes joy when I praise Him as I flick on my blinker and glide into that lined asphalt space.

I may not lay out a fleece and ask for Him to rain on it to demonstrate whether I should parallel park on the street or continue into the parking garage, but I do often ask for an extra tangible reminder of His prompting in the depths of my pain and in the heights of my joy. My God shows up, and He shows off.

In school, teachers often prompt students to put on their "listening ears" as an encouragement to hear the teacher's instructions. As believers, it's imperative for our "listening ears" to be in tune with the voice of the Lord's instructions.

In Judges 6, Gideon said to God, "'If You will save Israel by my hand as You have said—look, I shall put a fleece of wool on the threshing floor; if there is dew on the fleece only, and it is dry on all the ground, then I shall know that You will save Israel by my hand, as You have said.'" And it was so. When he rose early the next morning and squeezed the fleece together, he wrung the dew out of the fleece, a bowlful of water. Then Gideon said to God, "'Do not be angry with me, but let me speak just once more: Let me test, I pray, just once more with the fleece; let it now be dry only on the fleece, but on all the ground let there be dew.' And God did so that night. It was dry on the fleece only, but there was dew on all the ground" (vv. 36–40 NKJV).

While testing God may seem irreverent, when Gideon insisted on laying out fleece and making a request for God to show off, he set an example of searching—truly seeking out—the commands of the Lord. In Gideon's case, God asked him to abandon his army of hundreds of thousands in favor of a mere three hundred soldiers to face an opposing force. Maybe God is asking you to release your fears about having a child. Maybe He's stirring in your heart to leave the security of a full-time job to stay at home with your children. Or maybe He is asking you to stay in your marriage and watch Him move. No matter what the circumstances may be, God's Word affirms to us that He will provide no matter what.

What fleece are you laying out before Him? How do you see Him providing for you in small details? He is Jehovah Jireh, the One who will provide.

Dear God, thank You for being a divine provider. Lord, You know my needs even before I do. You see my weaknesses and where I am lacking, and You strengthen and fill them. God, please open the eyes of my heart to see all the tiny provisions You make for me every single day.

/ˈfāth/

noun

1. allegiance to duty or a person; loyalty
2. belief and trust in and loyalty to God
3. something that is believed, especially with strong conviction

TWENTY-FOUR

FAITH

◆

*Now faith is confidence in what we hope for and
assurance about what we do not see.*

HEBREWS 11:1

In my late twenties, I decided I wanted to skydive, so I asked my dad, a former Navy pilot, if he would join me in my jump. He declined, replying that he would never jump out of a perfectly working airplane. Instead, I gathered a group of my friends and braved the day.

Words can't describe the exhilaration of floating through the air once I took that step away from the safety of the plane's interior (untethered and not even tandem). After my first jump, three of the four of us wanted to go back for a second jump, including me. That time I was the first to leap, landing without incident.

One of my friends lost radio signal inside his helmet and drifted away from the jump path. The last jumper's parachute didn't open, and he had to rely on his reserve chute to ensure his safety. Medics raced to both, and ultimately they arrived on the ground safely, but not without reluctance to ever jump again.

During the dive, we wore helmets that were wired to keep us verbally connected to an expert on the ground who instructed us to stay on a course that would guarantee the safest landing and signaled us when it was time to land.

"Toggle right . . . toggle left . . . target in sight." For those of us who believe in Jesus, we're jumping solo but are never directionless. We are hardwired to have a connection with our Pilot, who guides us clearly and safely.

As I stood gripping the exterior of the plane, I could see a wide expanse of ground below me, but not the actual spot where I was directed to land, yet I trusted what I'd been told and took a literal leap of faith into a freefall with that voice in my head. No matter what I encountered, I had the assurance that I would be okay. Without being tuned in to the pilot's voice, I would have drifted out of the assigned path. Similarly, when I ignore the Lord's signals, I often find myself in places I never intended to go.

When the ground seemed to be rushing toward me, and as I began to panic, a calm voice commanded me to pull the parachute. I landed gently.

Walking with the Lord doesn't mean that you won't encounter turbulence or a loss of altitude, but it does mean that He is directing your freefall and will catch you as you land.

When was the last time you stepped out in faith? What keeps you from living a faith-filled life?

Dear God, give me faith to trust what You say. I know that sight is the opposite of faith, so rather than asking You to show me what You want from me, I am going to take a step and trust that there will be firm ground beneath my foot. Lord, fortify me where I am weak, and give me a faith that glorifies You in my life to all those around me.

/'təch/

verb

1. to bring a bodily part into contact with, especially so as
    to perceive through the tactile sense
2. to put hands upon in any way or degree
3. to deal with; become involved with

TWENTY-FIVE

TOUCH

◆

She came up behind him and touched the edge of his cloak, and immediately her bleeding stopped.

LUKE 8:44

Have you ever seen the *Mona Lisa*? The original painting by Leonardo da Vinci is small, only thirty by twenty-one inches, and is set behind layers of security and glass. This legendary work of art seems huge when you see the image reprinted on screen savers, mouse pads, posters, or T-shirts. Currently residing in the Louvre, the masterpiece is visited each day by thousands of people crowding around, hoping for a glimpse of the timeless piece of art.

The thing about the *Mona Lisa*, Vincent van Gogh's *The Starry Night*, the Sistine Chapel ceiling, and other masterpieces is that they are kept out of the public's reach. One human touch could deteriorate and devalue these priceless creations.

God, the master Creator, sent His most valuable masterpiece to walk among the people, and one touch from Him would restore every broken place. In the parable told in Luke 8:40–56, one woman was so desperate to receive healing from Christ that she broke through crushing masses of people to simply touch the hem of Jesus' cloak and received the healing she was so eager to obtain.

If we are truly honest with ourselves, I believe we would find that our fear is blocking us from receiving the Master's touch in our own lives. Maybe we're afraid of hoping and being disappointed, or we're afraid of just how our lives might change and disrupt the status quo. But I believe that if we can touch the cloak of Jesus, we will experience supernatural healing—physically, emotionally, and spiritually.

No matter what the doctors' reports might say, what the test results reflect, or what percentages and odds define, we have a healer who needs only to touch us. Miracles happen, and they happen constantly. God is still in the miracle business, if we allow Him to use us in that way. I invite you right now to uncross your arms and open your hands to His touch and His mighty power today.

Why don't we seek Him today as urgently as the woman in Scripture did so long ago? Why don't we rush toward that single touch that brings life? Where do you need healing?

Jesus, I believe that Your healing touch restores life and health in a moment. Thank You for the miracles that You perform every day. I ask that You help us relinquish the fear that clouds our hearts and separates us from You. Give me the faith that would cause me to rush through crowds for one touch of Your cloak. Give me a passion for You that is so fervent that nothing would stop me from experiencing Your wonder. I trust in Your strength, might, and glory.

Patient

/ˈpā-shənt/

adjective

1. bearing pains or trials calmly or without complaint

2. not hasty or impetuous

3. steadfast despite opposition, difficulty, or adversity

TWENTY-SIX

PATIENT

◆

Be patient, therefore, brothers, until the coming of the Lord. See
how the farmer waits for the precious fruit of the earth, being
patient about it, until it receives the early and the late rains.

JAMES 5:7 ESV

The past decade has been both exhilarating and exhausting for me. Since I was a little girl, I've had a passion deep inside of me to paint. At the same time, I had an equal passion to be a wife and a mom of many children.

In my high school history class, my mind would wander as I doodled a fantasy wedding scene and scribbled the names of my future children. I earned a D in that class. It may not be a grade I'm proud of, but my four children and husband are blessings I am incredibly proud of.

One spring we were at the beach, enjoying a long bike ride along some magnificent paths. My son had done something that made me so angry, and as I pedaled among the Spanish moss and huge oak trees, I found myself feeling impatient and having a conversation with God. "What am I doing wrong as a mother, Lord? Why does he choose to disobey me?" As I looked up at one point, I saw the most amazing trees. Their trunks and roots twisted and turned, yet they were strong and solid, with every branch pointing upward.

Something about the trees helped me realize that I had done my job as a mother and will continue to do my job to plant seeds of righteousness in my children and entrust our heavenly Father to water and nurture and grow these amazing children into the incredible adults God created them to be—in His time.

There may be times when your situation seems hopeless. Children growing in an opposite direction than you were hoping, a marriage that seems fruitless, a relationship that, like kudzu, has overgrown its boundaries and is choking you. If you're anything like me, you might want things to change right now, today. But—like me with my children—God is asking you merely to be obedient in planting the seeds and patient while He tends to the garden.

What seeds are you sowing in this season? Is the soil you're cultivating fertile or barren? How are you seeing God tend your garden? Where in your life could you demonstrate patience?

Dear God, my prayer today is that even when the soil doesn't feel fertile, You will strengthen me to continue planting, and bolster my faith in You as I trust You to be the Master Gardener over my life, removing weeds and multiplying carefully sown seeds. Replace my impatience with gratitude and help me experience joy in the journey as I watch Your handiwork in my life.

Storm

/ˈstȯrm/

noun

1. a disturbance of the atmosphere marked by wind and usually by rain, snow, hail, sleet, or thunder and lightning

TWENTY-SEVEN

STORM

---◆---

"The rain came down, the streams rose, and the winds
blew and beat against that house; yet it did not fall,
because it had its foundation on the rock."

MATTHEW 7:25

One early morning I began journaling in the middle of a storm. All around me the rain was pouring, the thunder was pounding, and the lightning was striking disconcertingly close to home. Between the flashes and claps, there were pauses of peace and calm.

As the rains came down, and I thought back to the way water cleansed God's people in the desert, I meditated on my desire to live a pure, cleansed life, free from storms.

Unfortunately, storms do happen, and more often than not, they pop up suddenly and without warning. The night before this strong gale, I absorbed the most brilliant sunset, painted with God's brushstrokes dipped in magnificent shades of pink, watching in awe as the sun sank into the horizon.

There was no evidence of a storm coming. However, in the quick turn of a moment, the storm hit. As I lay awake and journaling, I wondered how equipped I am to weather these storms. How prepared am I for the onslaught of wind and rain coming without warning? Certainly, little squalls cross our path—soaking showers that give way to rainbows and brilliant sunlight. There are also those slow, gray drizzles that seem to settle in and saturate our spirits. Still others erode our hearts with their vicious violence and ferocity. In any case, I want to be prepared and equipped. I want to fortify the banks of my heart so they will stay firmly planted and not be washed away.

God promised me, just as He promised Noah—and you—that undoubtedly, no matter the intensity of the storm, He will cause the sun to reappear. He will stop the rain and silence the thunderous claps. He will push the clouds apart and reveal His peace and assurance over my life, if only I will cling to the hope that He gives us in Jesus, and the hope He spells out for us in His Word. When I cling, He quiets. The storms are momentary, but His love and grace for me are eternal.

Is there a storm or some sort of natural disaster that's shaking up your life? Today I invite you to find shelter in God's warm, sturdy embrace.

Dear God, thank You for calming the storms that assault my life. Thank You for Your promise to quiet the thunder. I ask today that as I brace for the storms ahead of me, I would look to You as my Captain and not be afraid of the lightning above me.

/ˈfä-(ˌ)lō/

verb

1. to go, proceed, or come after

2. to copy after; imitate

TWENTY-EIGHT

FOLLOW

---

*But Ruth replied, "Don't urge me to leave you or to turn back
from you. Where you go I will go, and where you stay I will stay.
Your people will be my people and your God my God."*

RUTH 1:16

Our family recently took a trip to Dallas to visit two of my three
daughters for parents' weekend at college and to celebrate our eldest turning twenty-one. It may sound cliché, but it does truly feel like yesterday
when the doctors were setting her in my arms and I was quietly studying her face,
memorizing every feature our Creator had so beautifully sculpted, just for her, as
a perfect reflection of Himself and of Clark and me.

I always get emotional reading the story of Ruth and Naomi's love for each
other and Ruth's devotion to her mother-in-law, beseeching Naomi to allow her
to stay with her and promising her that wherever she went, Ruth would surely
follow. Actually, these lines also remind me of the Carole King song, "Where you
lead, I will follow, anywhere . . ."[1]

As a mother, I am struck by these words in two areas. First, my prayer as a
mother is not just that my children would want to follow the example I'm setting for them, but even weightier, I pray that I am walking down a road that they

should follow. I want to leave a legacy for them of character, integrity, grace, humility, forgiveness, generosity, wisdom, truth, and love.

Second, as I read Ruth's words to Naomi, I have to examine whether my heart is genuinely submitted to God in the same way. "Lord, do I truly want to go where You go? Am I willing to make the people You put before me my people? Am I truly placing my feet firmly in the footprints You have walked ahead of me?"

Ruth's devotion is inspiring. For Naomi, it was heavy with responsibility. And as both a mother and a follower of Christ, it's convicting.

Whose footsteps are you following?

Who is following *you*?

What example or legacy are you hoping to leave for those following you?

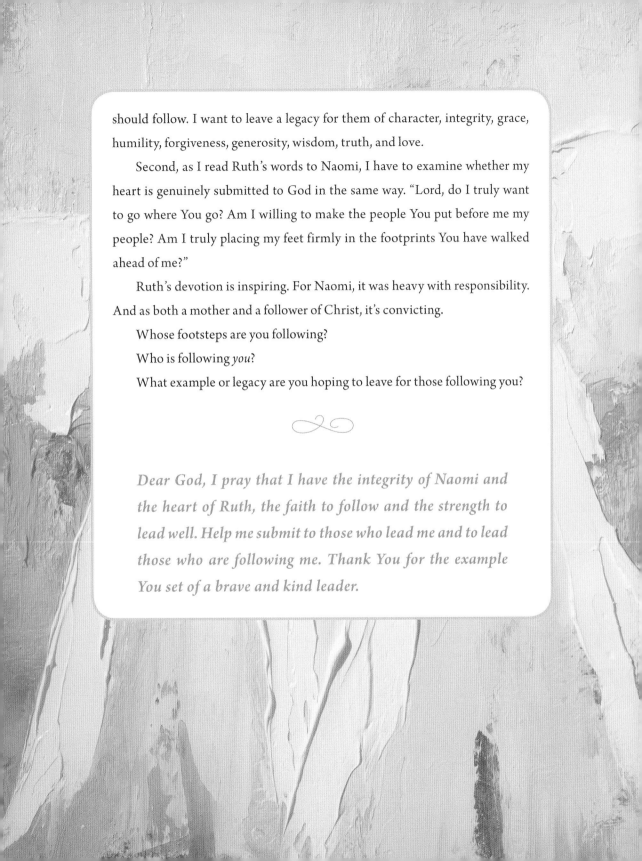

Dear God, I pray that I have the integrity of Naomi and the heart of Ruth, the faith to follow and the strength to lead well. Help me submit to those who lead me and to lead those who are following me. Thank You for the example You set of a brave and kind leader.

/ˈpath-ˌwā/

noun

1. a path; course

TWENTY-NINE

PATHWAY

*"But small is the gate and narrow the road that
leads to life, and only a few find it."*

MATTHEW 7:14

R oads are a hallmark setting for miraculous scenes and amazing examples in the Bible—from Mary's long, laborious ride down the roads into Bethlehem, Jesus' bittersweet journey along the Via Dolorosa to the cross, His walk down the road to Emmaus following His resurrection, and Saul's incredible conversion along the road to Damascus. In Jesus' day, roads were the breeding grounds for miracles.

Unfortunately, in my world, roads are more likely to serve as breeding grounds for headaches fueled by angst and fear if you are in the passenger seat with my husband at the wheel.

As much as I love my fine city of Charlotte, I can't help but notice that as I became more aware of the drivers around us, it is home to some of the rudest drivers, marked by impatience and aggression, enough to set any mother on edge with a new driver behind the wheel. When my youngest received his driver's permit several years ago, I kept assuring him that I wasn't as afraid of his abilities as I was fearful of the people around him and their potentially destructive decisions.

In the earliest years of our civilization, even the most mundane encounters could lead to the greatest miracles. Today we take for granted the power of our interactions. Our roads are a means of transportation, not a setting to display grace, hospitality, kindness, patience, or peace. It's unlikely that you will spit in dirt and rub mud on someone's eyes and restore their sight on a random Friday. But the streets and avenues you travel daily—both figuratively and literally—may still be a setting for God's mighty power to be highlighted.

I encourage you not to be distracted or caught up in the "traffic" of the world and of life, but instead travel on a freeway leading to a greater place. Let others merge with you.

Have you ever arrived at a destination on mental cruise control and wondered how you got there? When was the last time you let someone in—either on the road or in your lane of life? What pathways do you travel that lead you to destructive destinations, and how can you reset your personal GPS—your own "God Positioning System"—to help get you back on the right pathway?

Dear God, You have set pathways before me that may look scary. They may look bleak, but You have also carved out roads that promise to lead me alongside Your still waters. Lord, help me discern the direction You have set for me so that I don't wander away from Your will.

/ˈgu̇d-nəs/

noun

1. the quality or state of being good

2. the nutritious, flavorful, or beneficial part of something

THIRTY

GOODNESS

---◆---

I remain confident of this: I will see the goodness of the Lord
in the land of the living.

PSALM 27:13

I'm hoping that I'm not the only one who admits to occasionally talking to God as though He were the genie in *Aladdin*. Sadly, it's usually when I'm rubbing that lamp three times a day (okay, maybe only two, because I don't always bless my lunch) and making my requests unto Him.

"Lord," I say, oh so reverently, "my day has been really discouraging, and I'd really like for You to go ahead and fix all the people around me." (It's never me. It's always them.)

Shame on me for my flippant posture in those moments. In other seasons, my prayers and requests are deeper, beyond the mundane. They are fervent, full of emotion and authentic desperation. Whether for our kids' futures, the trajectory of our careers, the state of our marriages, wins for our team, or rallying around friends walking through infertility and pleading with God for children who aren't here—we want to be the recipients of God's goodness.

When God answers—and I can assure you that He always answers, whether or not it's the way we desire—I hope to always repeat the message from Daniel's life, which has become a popular quote based on a paraphrase of Daniel 3:1–24: "But if not . . . He is still good." If He does *not* answer the way I want Him to, He is still good. If we do *not* receive the news we want, He is still good.

There is such profound hope in the goodness of the Lord. It's assurance that even in the face of darkness and disappointment, His goodness reigns supreme. What sort of "nots" are currently gripping your spirit? I invite you to allow Him to penetrate and fortify your heart. He is still good, which means He always was and always will be.

Dear God, thank You for reminding me that You are good. Help me abandon my own expectations and instead fully acknowledge that whatever the outcome, you will work it for good. I pray that my attitude toward You is full of the same fervor in the despair as it is in the mundane and the triumphs. Thank You for Your kindness and the mercies that are available to me.

Scar

/ˈskär/

noun

1. a mark remaining after injured tissue has healed
2. a mark left where something was previously attached
3. a mark or indentation resulting from damage or wear
4. a lasting moral or emotional injury

THIRTY-ONE

SCAR

———————◆———————

He heals the brokenhearted and binds up their wounds.

PSALM 147:3

———————————————

We were well into a three-year process of building a new home for our family in the early 2000s—a process that challenged me and caused me to draw near to God in a new way. After crossing hurdles regarding whether to build or not, with drawing and pricing the plans, and with laying the foundation, we were eager to begin framing the house.

We continued seeking God's will in the process, and we pressed forward with construction. I was overjoyed to see the framing begin to shape our future home. Much to my dismay, when I visited our rapidly rising home, I found not-so-clean two-by-sixes and wood covered in knots—ugly wood that I argued surely couldn't build the strong house in which we were going to reside. I brought up my concerns with our builder. He simply told me, "Anne, the more knots there are in the timber, the stronger the wood is."

Along this process of building our home, and anytime I sought control or began to give in to my doubt, the Lord would nudge me and say, "Come back to Me." I couldn't have heard the words He spoke to my heart more deeply in response to my builder's explanation. "The more knots are in our lives, the stronger we are."

I was reminded of every trial, every battle, and every victory that was a mark on my heart, creating a knot and strengthening my spirit. I was encouraged that the knotty beams holding our house upright were similar to the scars that Jesus used to mark me and hold my life upright.

Once I embraced the marred timber, we claimed it in the Lord's name, inscribing scripture on the framing. I was deeply moved when, as a final step to seal the inner framework of our home, our construction crew came in and covered the wood with white drywall, covering the marks with a clean slate, exactly the way Jesus covered my knots by hanging on the cross. His blood that was shed was shed for me—all my knots, my sins, my scars. His covering was His righteousness, and what a beautiful picture is that!

The word *scar* isn't typically associated with something positive. However, I see things differently now, and I've come to value those places in my own life that show up as scars. How can you see some of your own scars as symbols of strength or victory?

Dear God, I know that You have allowed me to walk through fire for Your purpose. Help me not to hide my scars from those battles, but instead wear them with confidence so that all who see me will see Your glory and the victory You promised me.

/ˈshe-pərd/

verb

1. to guide and guard in the manner of a shepherd; a person who tends sheep

noun

1. a person who tends sheep

THIRTY-THREE

SHEPHERD

---◆---

Like a shepherd He will tend His flock, in His arm He will gather the
lambs and carry them in His bosom; He will gently lead the nursing ewes.
ISAIAH 40:11 NASB

One of my favorite names for God is Jehovah Rohi, which, translated, means "the Lord our Shepherd." As we studied about the Lord as our Shepherd, I had an image of God guiding us along His path, and I'd venture to say that it isn't our typical path.

Years ago, our family hiked the towns of Cinque Terre in Italy, which is the rugged portion of coastline on the Italian Riviera. It is composed of five villages. We were ambitious as a family and set out early one morning to hike all five lands. The hotel manager took one look at us and told us to take the train to the first two towns, skipping the hardest part and then hiking the rest. We all agreed that we could manage on our own and then set out on our way.

The beginning of the hike was steep and rocky. Five minutes into our journey, my husband and I were convinced we weren't going to make it. We rallied our spirits, got our acts together, and plodded forward.

When the path leveled, it also narrowed, with a steep drop-off on one side. There was not much to see in front of us because of the green brush surrounding the path, but we kept moving, putting one foot in front of the other.

This is much like our walk with the Lord as He guides us through life. Sometimes it may be steep or hard or rocky—or all three. Most always the path is narrow, for God's Word tells us in Matthew 7:13–14: "Enter through the narrow gate. For wide is the gate and broad is the road that leads to destruction, and many enter through it. But small is the gate and narrow the road that leads to life, and only a few find it."

Being on the hike with the steep, rocky parts and then on the narrow path, putting one foot in front of the other, we eventually rounded the bend to see the most breathtaking view you could imagine.

We have a God who loves us and who will guide us through anything that comes our way. Be it your marriage, finances, children, or health, hold fast to God's Word and His character—to the Good Shepherd. "Faith is the substance of things hoped for, the evidence of things not yet seen" (Hebrews 11:1 KJV)—the things that propel us to put one foot in front of the other.

What has God given you charge of? Who is in the flock you are called to shepherd? How can God help you lead them?

Thank You, Father, for watching over us and being our Shepherd, caring for each one of us. Should any of Your flock become lost, You are here to guide us back to safety. Father, You have entrusted me with my own flock of people in my life, and I ask for Your divine wisdom to help me shepherd each one with Your love and guidance.

/ri-ˈlēs/

verb

1. to set free from restraint, confinement, or servitude

THIRTY-FOUR

RELEASE

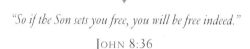

"So if the Son sets you free, you will be free indeed."
JOHN 8:36

It was a beautiful day at the beach. We were there for a girls' trip: my mom, my sister, and my three stepsisters. I had young children, whom I left back home with my husband, Clark, and I had promised them I would bring back a large cup of sharks' teeth.

I love the beach. I love walking on the beach, praising God for His mighty creation. There is such a calmness about hearing the ocean waves crash along the shore.

One morning, as I walked ahead of the group—praying, talking to God, and cleaning up the sharks' teeth—I became a little greedy and giddy about all the teeth I was collecting. Then I heard a still, small voice whisper: "Can you release these teeth that you have found?" I walked on and pretended I did not hear the stirring in my heart, but it grew louder and louder. "Can you release these, Anne?" After much arguing in my spirit, I knelt down and laid all the sharks' teeth in a neat little pile. I was disappointed, knowing that my sister would come up behind me and think she'd hit the jackpot with all these teeth.

As I looked up, I saw the most incredible conch shell about a foot ahead of me. This type of shell isn't common on Ponte Vedra Beach, only small crushed shells and sharks' teeth. I was stunned. When I picked it up, I heard that small voice again, speaking: "See? When you surrender, when you trust Me, when you are obedient to Me, see what I will do?"

I took the shell home, and it became a great reminder that when we release our attachments, when we let go and let God work in our life, we are set free from being confined to a limited way of thinking, as He can do so much more than we ever could imagine. The conch shell stayed next to my kitchen sink. It served as a daily reminder to always listen to His voice, to trust and obey, and to watch what God can do in our lives.

Is God calling you to release something? Is He calling you to surrender something that's no longer serving you? Can you see where surrendering and trusting in the past has led to something greater?

Dear God, help me hear Your voice. Lord, letting go and releasing our desires and attachments can be so hard. My sinful nature may want me to abandon and avoid hardships, but I ask that You give me strength to follow You passionately into the wild.

Prayer

/ˈprer/

noun

1. an address (such as a petition) to God or a god in word or thought

2. an earnest request or wish

THIRTY-FIVE

PRAYER

◆

*Pray in the Spirit on all occasions with all kinds of prayers and requests. With
this in mind, be alert and always keep on praying for all the Lord's people.*

Ephesians 6:18

I dislike the words *religion* and *religious*. For me, faith is having
a relationship with a living God who wants to have a personal
relationship with me—not some type of rote performance.

God loves me. He sees me and knows everything I ever go through—the
ups and the downs. He wants me to cry out to Him when I am suffering and sad,
and He wants me to rejoice and give thanks to Him when I am joyful and happy.

Any kind of relationship requires personal communication to maintain that
relationship, especially if you desire any level of quality intimacy.

Prayer is just that: communicating with a living person in the form of Jesus.
Trusting with all of your heart, mind, and soul. Being comforted by that person.
Being guided by that person. Being held by that person.

I was introduced to prayer as a young child. But it wasn't until I was introduced to God's Word—the Bible—that prayer became the foundation of my
relationship with Jesus. God's Word is living and active and sharper than any
double-edged sword (Hebrews 4:12). It penetrates to the very heart of the matter
and cuts through any lies that the world would have us believe.

More than anything, God's ultimate desire for us is to have a personal relationship with Him. How do we do that? By simply talking. Not only at night before we go to bed. Or only in the morning at the breakfast table. But all throughout our days. In the midst of our worry, and in the midst of our joys.

I have an acronym for the word *prayer* that I hope will resonate with you:

Position yourself. Do you have a relationship with Jesus? Have you surrendered your life to Him, or asked Him to be your Lord and Savior?

Repent. Turn from anything not in line with God's Word. Ask Him daily to cleanse your heart and renew your spirit.

Acknowledge that He is sovereign. He is always there. He sees you.

Yield to the Holy Spirit. God gave us a gift in the Holy Spirit. Quiet yourself from the noise of the world to hear His Spirit whisper.

Encourage. Build one another up through prayer and by praying for others.

Rejoice! First Thessalonians 5:16–18 tells us to "rejoice always, pray continually, give thanks in all circumstances."

How has the power of prayer played a role in your life?

Dear God, I pray that You would teach me how to deepen my own prayers with You. Instill in me that knowing, that desire for constant communication with You, in my ups and my downs, when I'm being obedient and serving You at my highest and best, and when I am not living in accordance with Your plan for me.

Entrust

/in-ˈtrəst/

verb

1. to commit to another with confidence

THIRTY-SIX

ENTRUST

◆

Entrust your work to the LORD, and your planning will succeed.

PROVERBS 16:3 ISV

My husband and I had somewhat of a fairy-tale courtship. It was during a time when I had totally surrendered my life over to the Lord, walking in His will, trusting that He would bring me a husband at His appointed time, not mine. Clark and I were set up on a blind date in June 1993. He and I had about ten dates over the course of two months. That August, he invited me to the beach to meet his parents and spend time over the weekend. I remember that Saturday, sitting at the beach in the surf with my prayer sheets, praying for friends and family members. As I watched the tide roll in and out, I heard the Lord ask me, "What do you want in a mate? What are your expectations?" My reply was that I wanted someone who loved the Lord, who was kind, and who had a great sense of humor. I heard the Lord whisper back, "Are you ready to trust Me?"

Forty-eight hours later, Clark sat across from me, saying, "I love you. I want to take care of you for the rest of my life. Will you marry me?"

Wow. That was quick, Lord!

Twenty-six years later, we have four children and live a full, active life. I always wanted a big family, and I absolutely love the life we've built together and the four gifts God entrusted to us. Life was physically exhausting and demanding, but we pressed on, knowing that life was also precious. As parents, we so wanted them to be happy, to make good decisions, and to be compassionate toward others.

My job as their mother both then and now is to sow seeds of God's truth into their hearts as often as possible. My eldest daughter went off to boarding school in the tenth grade, and I was devastated that someone else would be involved in raising my child on a daily basis. When I got home and spent time with the Lord, He reminded me of that day on the beach.

During that time of reflection and surrender, the Lord had gently urged me to entrust my future marriage to Him, and He fulfilled that promise to me. Even more so, He reminded me that should I entrust these four treasures to Him, I didn't need to worry about who may be raising them, because they are all firmly nestled and entrusted to His mighty hand.

What have you been entrusted with? What are you entrusting to God? Take a moment to notice this mutual aspect of your relationship with God. The more we entrust to Him, the more He entrusts to us.

Dear God, today I commit to You those whom I love. Lord, I'm easily tempted to try to control their lives, believing that I know what is best for them. Instead, I recognize that You are the One who knows best. You have given me so many gifts in the people around me, and I ask that You speak truth, love, protection, and peace over them today.

Give

/ˈgiv/

verb

1. to make a present of
2. to grant or bestow by formal action
3. to accord or yield to another
4. to convey to another

THIRTY-SEVEN

GIVE

Each of you should give what you have decided in your heart to give,
not reluctantly or under compulsion, for God loves a cheerful giver.
2 CORINTHIANS 9:7

I have three daughters, and I have loved watching them grow and experiment with makeup, fashion, and perfume. I loved the way they smelled when they were younger, slathering on fruity-scented lotions. My girls are adults now and have a taste for more expensive fragrances. They have become quite savvy in the perfume and cosmetics department. There are certain perfumes and lotions that will always remind me of those early days with the girls becoming women, and we share a favorite perfume, Scent of Peace.

I am not as attuned to makeup know-how, and a few years ago, my eldest daughter commented that she was upset that I didn't teach them more about hair and makeup, and instead only taught them about God!

When Simon the leper hosted a dinner in Jesus' honor, a woman in attendance approached Jesus holding her dearest possessions. She enthusiastically and lavishly poured out her perfume on her Savior, anointing first His head and then His feet, weeping and wiping Him with her hair. What a beautiful picture of surrender at the feet of Christ!

This precious woman gave limitlessly to God all that she had. She broke her alabaster jar to release the treasure inside and sacrifice it for her King. I remember trying to teach my daughters restraint in those early days, and the disciples at this party did the same thing, scolding her for recklessly pouring out her goods when they could be sold to benefit the poor.

I'm so thankful for a God who embraces those who bow with humility and awe at His feet and who quiets the criticisms that assail our generosity. I am humbled by how this woman shared the entirety of her most valued gifts for the benefit of Christ. Am I pouring out all that I have for His glory? Do I treat God more like Simon the leper: opening my door for Him to come in, but not greeting Him with a kiss, an anointing, a sacrificial gift? I think my heart tends to be positioned like Simon, feeling like my open door is enough, taking His presence for granted in my home.

I love that God encourages audacious giving. He is a God of multiplication, and He takes our gifts and increases them for His glory.

What do you hold most dear that you could share with God? What do you hold precious that you could pour out in His name and for His glory?

Dear God, please help me find my alabaster jar—my most precious gift and offering. More than that, give me the audacity to break it wide open as a sacrifice before Jesus, anointing Him with the oil of my finest perfume without a thought of the cost. You have given me so much, and today I return it to You.

Seek

/ˈsēk/

verb

1. to go in search of; to look for

2. to try to discover

3. to ask for; request

THIRTY-EIGHT

SEEK

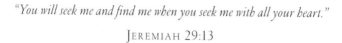

"You will seek me and find me when you seek me with all your heart."

JEREMIAH 29:13

There are days when life seems to be clicking right along seamlessly. The kids aren't fighting, the house is clean, work gets done, and there aren't any glitches in the day. Then there are days that you don't quite know what happened, with bumps and interruptions all day long—short tempers, strewn laundry, disgruntled children. I have learned that when I seek God first in all I do, my days are much more peaceful.

My daughter Catherine was about nine years old when she lost a little black stuffed animal at church one Sunday. Catherine shed many tears as the church's halls and classrooms were searched, and we still couldn't find our lost stuffed dog. We prayed that God would help us find it. Nights became difficult as a result of her losing the little animal, but eventually we found another one for her to snuggle with and all was well.

A few weeks later, during morning prayer time in the chapel at our church— deep in prayer for our clergy, our family, and people in need—I felt a slight interruption and urge to pray for the lost stuffed dog. I felt silly. I mean—there are so many more important things to pray for. But I felt the urge again, so I gave in and prayed for the lost dog. When I was finished, I packed up my things and headed to the car until I felt a nudge to head to the front office. I had a busy day ahead, and I almost dismissed the nudge for more important things to do.

Instead, I headed to the office and asked Stella, the receptionist, if there were any other places in the church that had a lost and found. She asked what I was looking for, and when she heard, she opened her bottom drawer and pulled out the little black dog. Attached was a note to call the little girl who had found the dog by 10:00 a.m. on a specific date if it had not been claimed. I happened to show up at 9:50 a.m. on that date.

I left the church with dog in hand and a very important message pressed on my heart: No matter what, seek God in all things and for all things. Pray without ceasing for the big things in my life, as well as the small things. Even though we don't always get answers to our prayers right when we want them or *think* we need them, God is always in control and always right on time.

What is God saying yes to in your life and where is He saying no or "not yet"? Sometimes we need to wait and ask again or ask a different way. Can you see how God's divine timing is sometimes a reminder for us to be present to miracles?

Dear God, today my prayer is neither singular nor temporary. Let my prayer today open up an eternal dialogue as I seek You at all times. Let my "amen" not be the end of our conversation, but a time of reflection in our relationship together.

Forgive

/fər-ˈgiv/

verb

1. to cease to feel resentment against; pardon
2. to grant relief from payment of

THIRTY-NINE

FORGIVE

Be kind and compassionate to one another, forgiving
each other, just as in Christ God forgave you.

EPHESIANS 4:32

My husband, Clark, and I are grateful to have a marriage that is a partnership, based on godly love, friendship, and shared experiences. But while thinking about writing this entry on forgiveness, some ugly memories surfaced. Early in our marriage (and quite frankly, throughout), we would argue. As with most spats, neither of us can remember how one particular argument started, but it turned nasty quickly. We both became angry. Impassioned by our pride and the flares of emotion, we wanted to pack it up, cut our losses, and walk away. (Sometimes it seems so easy to walk away rather than tend to the mess.)

As I lay there stewing in the dark, making every effort not to cross the invisible battle line we'd drawn in the bed, I knew I needed to forgive Clark even if my heart wasn't quite there yet. Whenever I feel wronged, I slip into martyrdom and back away, often hurling out revenge with my resentful silence. But really, I'm just encasing myself in a prison, shutting out even God, who so desperately wants to give me freedom from my injuries and soothe my ruffled, inflamed heart.

Often, the injuries aren't just small nicks across the plains of our emotions.

They can consist of wounds that twist and wind around our very core, caused by the trauma of abuse, betrayal, or crime. These events are extremely difficult to navigate; finding your way to the freedom from pain that God is holding out to you isn't always easy or obvious.

Forgiveness is a process to unpack our most shameful and tender hurts, and to trust a Lord who already knows. The wonderful thing about our Father is that He doesn't simply offer sympathy and a pitying smile. He *knows*. He can empathize with every slight and injustice. He experienced betrayal, loss, and physical abuse. He is there in your suffering, because He already endured it on your behalf. Even more beautifully, He has already forgiven *you* for the pain you've inflicted on others and the sins you have committed against Him.

Forgiveness requires sacrificial fellowship. It implores you to clean up the messes made daily by others wreaking havoc on your fragile heart. With God, however, the messes aren't our responsibility. A spirit inclined to forgive and give up the bitterness is all we need. Healing doesn't always happen immediately, but it's happening even as you read this. The scabs can soften, the wounds can close, and the scars can fade. The freedom is yours.

Is there someone you need to forgive? Or a situation for which you need to ask forgiveness? Right around the corner is a great freedom waiting for you.

Dear God, You know the hurts I have stored up and the anger I refuse to release. You have forgiven me for so much, and I ask that my heart be softened to do the same for those who have hurt me. Thank You for Your never-ending forgiveness.

Purpose

/ˈpər-pəs/

noun

1. something set up as an object or end to be attained; intention

FORTY

PURPOSE

---◆---

*We know that for those who love God all things work together
for good, for those who are called according to his purpose.*

ROMANS 8:28 ESV

I never envy the administrative staff at the doctor's office, the hair salon, or (shudder) the DMV, where I recently spent some time. Each of these places lines up appointments one after the next in an orderly fashion, yet they also bear the brunt of the fallout when that order self-destructs into chaos, complaints, delays, and personal emergencies.

As we wear the carpets of our lives threadbare with constant pacing, we may miss out on the miracle appointed for that day. Sometimes God has appointed us to be the ones calling others back. He is constantly arranging His people into positions to be used for His higher purpose.

One day, I was in a department store, hurriedly trying to cross some gifts off my shopping list, while also scrolling through my phone and inventorying the texts, voice mails, and emails coming in. The salesclerk noticed my wedding ring and told me how much she loved it. I politely thanked her and looked back at my phone, caught up in my own schedule. I heard her ask me if I knew the secret to a long and happy marriage. Bemused, I glanced up and back down, and then finally tuned in to the Spirit telling me to put down my phone. I immediately noticed how beautiful she was and listened with a heavy heart as she told me about the divorce she was walking through. As we spoke, I was able to minister to her and later sent her a copy of my previous book, *Angels in Our Midst*, to encourage her weary spirit.

God reminded me about listening to His voice. He used what would have been another mundane transaction in my day as a divine appointment, allowing this woman to feel heard and listened to. I had a new purpose that day, one I didn't even know about when I woke up that morning.

God is a master scheduler. He makes divine appointments and sets us on collision courses with His master calendar. Meanwhile, there's a whole world around us for us to engage in. There's a purpose to the delayed appointments, and even a purpose to talking with strangers.

November 10? You might just have an appointment with destiny that day. Or maybe tomorrow. Or maybe a month from now. Or maybe not for another fourteen years. He has a date circled on His calendar designated just for you.

What are some of the divine appointments from your past that you can recall God scheduling for you? What are some of the purposes God has put on your heart that have surprised you?

Dear God, I'd like to think that I know what I'm doing today, but the truth is—I don't. I don't know what all I'm doing today or whom I will meet, but I ask that You shift my perspective to be a holy one so that no matter who or what I encounter, I will see You in it.

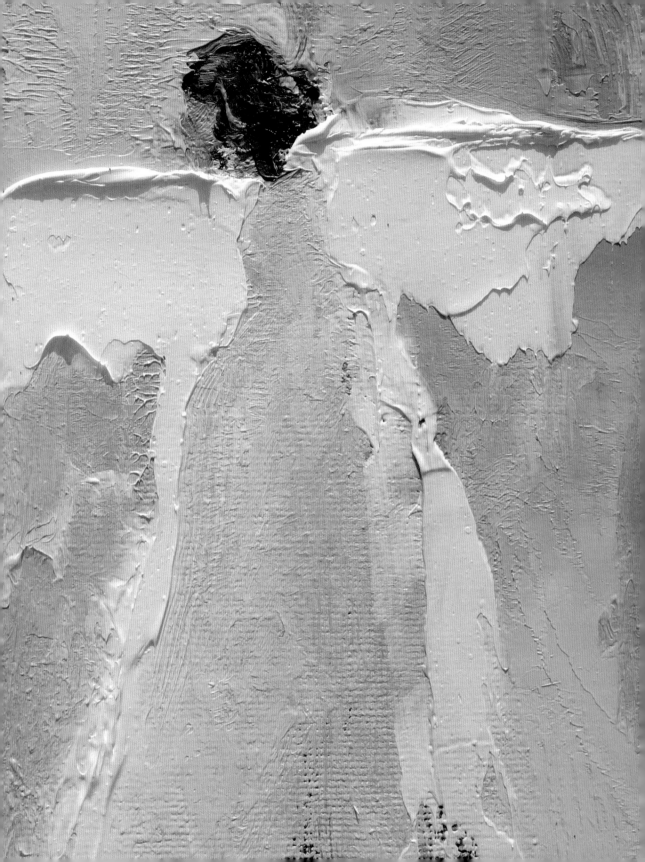

ACKNOWLEDGMENTS

*I*t has been such an amazing journey writing this little devotional. I have wanted to get this into your hands for years now and finally we have a small little book of "angels" and encouraging words to guide you through life's journey.

God's Word tells us in Psalm 100:4–5 to "enter His gates with thanksgiving and His courts with praise, give thanks to Him and praise His name." God gets the first bit of praise for this little book. He deposited in me at a young age this deep desire and dream to be an artist. He even deposited the dream to write, even though I mix up words and butcher the English language at times! But God is faithful and gets all the glory for this devotional. These are His words spoken through me—a broken individual who has seen His redemptive glory shine through.

Next comes my family. Although they really did not even know about the process of writing this book, they stand by my side daily bringing encouragement even in the midst of family drama, trials, and storms. I am grateful for God's grace that weaves through the crazy dynamics within our family. And my mom; moms are the most important people in our lives and I am grateful for the legacy that my mom continues to instill in each of us: the power of prayer! The power of His living Word!

When the stirring in my heart began to bubble about writing and publishing this

---

ABOUT THE AUTHOR

Anne Herring Neilson is well-known for her ethereal Angel Series, which are inspiring reflections of her faith, recognized for their stunning use of color. In response to demand for more access to her acclaimed Angel paintings, Neilson published two coffee-table books and launched Anne Neilson Home, a growing collection of luxury home products, including candles, notecards, Scripture cards, prints, and journals. Neilson also owns Anne Neilson Fine Art, a gallery located in Charlotte, North Carolina. Representing more than fifty talented artists from around the world, the gallery is dedicated to being a lighthouse, illuminating the work of both emerging and established artists.

As a wife, mother of four, artist, author, and philanthropist, Anne paints and creates with passion and purpose, always giving back to others by contributing to local, national, and international charitable organizations.

Learn more about Anne, her artwork, and Anne Neilson Home products at anneneilsonhome.com.